CHAPLAINS
Ministers of Hope

Edited by Alan Hilliard
Foreword by Bishop Éamonn Walsh

Published by Messenger Publications, 2021

ISBN 9781788125109

Scripture quotations from New Revised Standard Version Bible unless otherwise stated,
National Council of the Churches of Christ in the United States of America,
used by permission. All rights reserved worldwide.

Designed by Messenger Publications Design Department
Typeset in Garamond Premier Pro
Printed by W & G Baird Ltd

Messenger Publications,
37 Leeson Place, Dublin D02 E5V0
www.messenger.ie

This book is dedicated to the late Fr Gerry Byrne, priest of the Archdiocese of Dublin and chaplain to the Blackrock Clinic from 1986 to 2020.

Thank You

Alan Hilliard

I would like to acknowledge the commitment of so many in making this publication possible. The initial meetings with Éamonn Walsh and Donal Neary SJ ensured that the idea was always more than mere talk. Their partnership and encouragement in this project has allowed the idea to flourish into this publication. I wish to thank those in the Messenger office who gave immediate welcome to the idea, the framework and the book – your eagerness to publish was a great incentive to pursue the idea and to work to the timeline you laid out. How we hate timelines but how necessary they are! Thanks are due to Cecilia West, Director of Messenger Publications, Fiona Biggs and Kate Kiernan for their editorial work, Paula Nolan for her design and layout and Carolanne Henry for her work in publicising this publication.

Thank you to all the contributors. The words of love and inspiration from those who knew Gerry are a wonderful way to start the book. Chaplaincy begins and ends with human beings who work together to allow God's infinite grace to manifest itself. A special word of gratitude to John McCarthy and Tom Grenham who, while writing for this publication, faced the loss of loved ones. We remember John's mother Sheila and Tom's brother-in-law Gerry in our prayers.

To those of you who contributed to Part Two: I know you are very busy people in your own lives, but the fact that you were willing to contribute chapters of such high standard is both humbling and affirming. You have succeeded in raising chaplaincy to a new level within the mission of the Church. Your contributions may enlighten those who are charged with missioning to re-evaluate the support and the resources for these various roles.

To all of you who contributed from your front-line experience: Many of you had never written for a publication such as this before. If this book has achieved nothing else it has highlighted that we need to pay more attention to those of you who are making a difference but say very little about your work. I found your insights, your stories and the nourishment you received in your work to be a source of encouragement and enthusiasm in my own ministry. Please continue to write, to inspire.

While this book started out as a tribute to the late Fr Gerry Byrne the journey has been interesting. We have discovered that the book will not only be a testament to his life but will live on in courses that educate and nurture pastoral theologians and chaplains in the future. This will *happen* not only because a publication such as this one is a first, but because it combines a delicate balance of front-line work, deeply held conviction and a generous framework from which to view this incredible ministry of hope.

Thank you to the management, staff and patients of the Blackrock Clinic for providing Gerry with a place to minister during his priestly life. Thank you also for the interest you have shown in this publication and for agreeing to host its launch.

Finally, thank you to those of you who don't know that this book is published and who have become part of its most special moments: those of you who sat with a chaplain in a cell, on a boat, beside a hospital bed, in a hostel, in a foreign land, in an office or on a street, whether you spoke or signed or just remained quiet. Without doubt, in the circumstances of life that you faced, you were the ones who challenged us to never to give up and always to hope in things beyond us.

Contents

Part One
Fr Gerry Byrne: A Minister of Hope

Part Two
Perspectives of Hope

Part Three
Places of Hope

'The first priority for the chaplain, whether priest, religious or layperson, is to bring and show God's compassion to those in need.'

WORDS OF FR GERRY FROM A TALK TO THE MEMBERS OF LEGATUS (DUBLIN CHAPTER) ENTITLED 'HOSPITAL CHAPLAINCY AND ITS FUTURE ROLE', 10 MARCH 2015.

Foreword

It is indeed an honour and a joy to write the foreword to this book. As an auxiliary bishop in Dublin for over thirty years I have witnessed at first hand the outstanding contributions that chaplains make to individuals, the institutions in which they work, the Church and society. I am overjoyed that the rich diversity of the mission is captured in these pages in such a reflective, soulful and academic manner. It is hard to understand why a publication such as this was not on the shelves before now.

This is a real must-buy. Most definitely it is an 'Add to Cart' book. The contributions are practitioners and theologians. All those who have contributed to this book are eminently qualified in their field and offer an insight into the joy of their mission and an understanding of their role. The choice of the contributors by the editor is inspiring, and their written reflections are even more inspiring, as you will find out when you read through these pages. Readers will be enriched by a wide range of contributions from experienced chaplains from the worlds of prison, migration, education, healthcare, army, homelessness and hospice among others.

This publication is both timely and needed. It is a most welcome contribution to those who are both a part of the world of chaplaincy or are considering becoming a part of chaplaincy at some time in the future. These pages contain information that I consider to be compulsory reading for anyone interested in chaplaincy, be they practitioner, student, lecturer, work colleague or, indeed, anyone searching for deeper meaning in life. This publication provides a historical, scriptural, theological and pastoral background to chaplaincy while being true to its Christian roots and origins.

Chaplaincy in an immense variety of its expressions is to be found in these pages. It will interest those among you with an academic interest as well as being a solid practitioner's guide. In a gentle, non-threatening way it addresses life's big questions through real situations while providing fruitful stimulation for those coping with challenges of ill health, shattered dreams and living away from home, and for those standing at many of the crossroads of life. As well as being a valuable resource for those in the eye of the storm and their families and friends, it is an easy read that gives great accessibility to such important issues that emerge in people's lives.

The book traces the ecclesiastical historical development of chaplaincy from being financially dependent on the lord of the manor who could dismiss you in an instant should he or his household object to the content of a sermon, to the present-day prophetic role of the chaplain who is at times called to be the voice of the unpopular truths. The late Bishop Augustine Harris, Bishop of Middlesbrough and a former senior Roman Catholic prison chaplain, tells the story of a prison chapel where there was a live cannon accompanied by a guard with a lighted torch ready to fire it at the congregation should they lack due attention to or reverence for the liturgy. Any disturbance threatened to blow the prisoners into the kingdom the preacher was so eloquently referencing in his homily. Today that chapel is still equipped with the live cannon, the only difference now being that the chaplain is in the line of fire!

Another reason that gives me great joy to contribute to this publication is that it is dedicated to a great friend and colleague of mine, the late Fr Gerry Byrne. Gerry taught me that something that can at first appear to be a devastating setback in life can often turn one's life in a new direction that provides countless blessings for others and for one's self. This is well illustrated in his life.

When working on the land, a tractor went into reverse in error, and the young, vibrant sixteen-year-old boy, Gerry Byrne, standing on the back of that tractor was pinned against the wall. The accident interrupted schooling, led to surgery and lengthy hospitalisations. The consultant who detected latent multiple sclerosis wisely discerned constant monitoring, rather than conveying the bad news unnecessarily to one on the threshold of his life. He sensed Gerry was considering priesthood. Remaining a lifelong friend and physician, he felt vindicated when he attended Gerry's ordination. Following his ordination, Archbishop Ryan asked Gerry what his appointment preferences would be. 'Hospital chaplaincy' was Gerry's reply. When asked to expand he cited his experience as a teenager in Cappagh and Richmond Hospitals. Smiling, the Archbishop said, 'I will do what I can in the context of diocesan needs.' This followed an appointment as curate in Palmerstown and chaplain to Stewart's Hospital, which resulted in six glorious years of priestly enthusiasm. In that setting Gerry's wit and straight talking brought much fun and joy, both to himself and to those he served.

During his time at Palmerstown, what presented as a dental referral was quickly diagnosed as trigeminal neuralgia, leading to brain surgery, and the numbing news that this was the first sign of his MS becoming active. Sitting him down, his consultant unfolded what had first appeared over fifteen years earlier. He had always said, 'Gerry, you will age early but will have a full life.' Following this Gerry's area bishop, Donal Murray, encouraged him to become a full-time hospital chaplain. He subsequently enrolled in the clinical pastoral chaplaincy course at St Vincent's Hospital and upon successful graduation he was appointed chaplain to the newly opened Blackrock Clinic in 1986 where he served until his death on 26 May 2020. A winding road to Blackrock – was it chance, destiny or something more? Fr Gerry spent thirty-four years ministering in the clinic where he faced the same questions with patients that he had to face in his own life. One thing is certain, and this is seen in Gerry's life and throughout this publication – you have to play the hand life deals you regardless of your beliefs.

Listening to feedback from those who have been served well over the years I can honestly say that chaplains often do not fully realise the impact of their life's work. That line from scripture rings through – 'By their fruits you shall know them.' The words summarising Fr Gerry's ministry and his impact can be addressed to so many chaplains who do outstanding work on a daily basis.

In a world that measures success in material and monetary terms, the chaplain often swims against the cultural tide of image and flawless achievement, where there is no room for imperfection. The filter of today's world does not tolerate mistakes. A world of name, blame and shame has been created while the world of recovery is one of rebuilding lives where one names the issue, claims it by taking responsibility for what is to hand, and through grace and the kindness of others seeks to tame what formerly caused hurt and discontent. This book helps us to see the beauty, truth and strength of the Church's counter-cultural message. This publication reveals how chaplains allow the Risen Lord to work through them, to use their humanity and belief, as the instruments of Christ's love, wisdom, mercy and compassion in an often broken and imperfect world. I commend this book to you as you try to understand and unfold your own mission and purpose in our world.

Bishop Éamonn Walsh
Auxiliary Bishop Emeritus of Dublin

Introduction

Alan Hilliard

'I wish someone had told me about the chaplains earlier in my time at college … I wouldn't have had to carry so much on my own.' These were the words of a final-year student in a third-level setting. Having borne so much on her own due to family alienation she discovered the chaplaincy service during her last few months of college. During her final months we walked together through many difficulties until she graduated.

For many years chaplains have been left to 'get on with it', and they have done so heroically in many cases. They fill gaps, step into storms and are generally available to serve those that come to them in ways that are affirming and imaginative. Today there is more scrutiny. There are some who scrutinise because they scrutinise everything from a 'value for money' perspective, and there are some who scrutinise because they want to rid society of everything that has faith-based motivation.

This book is timely because it lets those who are involved in this valuable work scrutinise and give expression to what they do, why they do it and why they keep doing it. The book started with a conversation with Éamonn Walsh following the death of one of the longest-serving chaplains in the Archdiocese of Dublin, Fr Gerry Byrne. Covid-19 made it very difficult to say goodbye to him due to the restrictions on the number of people who could attend funerals; we all know only too well the pain of parting and the pain of not being able to be there for others during that parting. The book became a platform to showcase not only his caring and compassionate presence but that of so many others in a variety of settings.

'I'm not religious' is probably the most common opening sentence that chaplains hear in their engagements with people. Once this is out of the way the real work happens. The engagement between human beings who lighten one another's journey is often the most privileged moment that one can countenance. The first short section of the book gives a vignette of Gerry's outreach in the hospital and his engagement with patients and staff. The second section comprises an academic exploration of chaplaincy from the perspective of various disciplines, and the third and final section of the book looks at the extraordinary work of chaplains at the coalface of life and ministry.

We are most fortunate to have gathered some of Ireland's finest theologians and educationalists to help us reflect in Part Two on the larger issues facing chaplaincy today. Eugene Duffy's chapter sets the tone of the conversation by asking if chaplaincy deserves more recognition and status within the mission of the Church. The remaining contributions reference the growth and development of chaplaincy over the centuries, how it is consolidated today, and the current challenges facing chaplaincy and how these might be addressed. The historical, ecclesial, scriptural, educational and sociological elements are woven into this section to show the value and importance of this ministry of hope.

Part Three provides a wonderful tapestry of the range of chaplaincies and the incredible human encounters that occur in day-to-day ministry. Some of the contributions dwell more on the outcomes for those who are served, while others look more deeply at why a chaplain chooses to do this work. There are touching scenes of moments with the homeless, those who are dying, those who are recovering, those living away from home, those in prison, those on the front line of peace-keeping or in an educational setting. All these moments are about facilitating others to be who they need to be in moments of adversity or moments of joy. Yes, as the title says, chaplaincy is about hope but, as this books shows, it is also about human flourishing, both for the chaplains and for those they serve.

Some may feel more comfortable reading Part Three first to get a greater sense of the practical work of chaplains, but wherever you start, all the contributions will help you to discern views or even answers to the questions raised in Eugene Duffy's opening chapter. Those in chaplaincy often feel that they are at the periphery of the Church. They are at the periphery of life but there is often little support and direction for their work. Talk of being part of the 'mission' of the Church is often vague and lacks real dialogue. Reports are written but there is often no feedback or critique, leaving many chaplains wondering if their reports are even read. The theory and practice outlined so graciously in the individual contributions within this publication unknowingly challenge this malaise.

Part One

Fr Gerry Byrne: A Minister of Hope

1: A Family Member's Perspective

Karla Clarke Hanley

I met Gerry in 1997 in Blackrock Clinic, a sad time for my family as my dad was dying of cancer. Gerry and Dad became close over the few months he spent there, I have no doubt discussing rugby amongst other things. I know my dad was extremely fond of Gerry, how could he not be? Gerry celebrated the Last Rites with dad and he sat with the whole family, comforting and offering endless support to us all. This is where our friendship started. Gerry realised I needed help, and he reached out. Gerry became a bridge to my healing and ultimately a true and wonderful friend.

He was just there; he listened, and he cared. There was no preaching. Despite my objections at times, Gerry brought me back. He renewed my faith. He was kind, a listener, and always had a gem of advice. The advice could be heeded or not, and it was never forceful – nothing forceful.

Gerry was benevolent. Every year since my dad passed away, he celebrated Dad's anniversary mass. When there were tears Gerry would acknowledge the sadness, smile and say, 'This too will pass'. The Mass became a tradition that proved very supportive. Simply put, as a chaplain Gerry cared. He was a true friend, there for me at the worst time of my life. Even during his own illness, he said Mass for my dad in his beautiful home in Balbriggan. I did not know it was to be the last anniversary Mass he would celebrate for my dad. Doesn't that say everything about my dear friend – always thinking of others.

It was through Gerry I got to meet his wonderful family, Breda, Mary and Jane. We had many beautiful afternoons in Balbriggan looking out over the stunning garden having wonderful chats. Again, seeing the kind, caring person Gerry was and the love and fun that was shared in the house was intoxicating. It was here in the beautiful garden in Balbriggan that I learned of Gerry's love of daffodils.

Gerry had many friends. They seemed to be endless. Walking with him was like walking around with the greatest and the best. Everyone knew him and everyone wanted to talk to him. This was especially true in the Blackrock Clinic where everyone knew Gerry. All the staff, the patients and families of patients. There was a never-ending queue of love for such a special man.

I vividly recall a time when my family attended Christmas Mass in Blackrock Clinic and my son, who was eight at the time, fainted in the front row. Gerry's instinct was to come to the rescue. He immediately paused the ceremony and located a glass of water. You could feel the whole congregation respect his humanity, selflessness and kindness in a moment such as this.

His memory lives on in so many of us that he touched. Gerry, a true friend, a gentleman, non-judgemental, humanitarian, fun, considerate, compassionate, kind, devout, dedicated to his family and friends; he always had a special place for those he knew who were in need.

It's impossible to put into words how much Gerry's priesthood and friendship meant to me. Gerry changed my outlook on life and he gave without expecting anything in return. I gained a friend; one I will never forget and whom I miss greatly.

Daffodils are one of Gerry's favourite flowers. When I see daffodils bloom my dear friend is everywhere, bringing me fun and smiles countrywide. When you see a daffodil, remember Gerry, the bright, fun-loving and caring person he was and always will be – a loved treasure.

2: A Consultant's Perspective

James M. Sheehan

I was so privileged to meet Fr Gerry Byrne when the Blackrock Clinic opened in 1984 and he was appointed as our full-time chaplain by Archbishop Dermot Ryan. Fr Gerry was then a youthful priest but had received his own heavy cross. He had recently been diagnosed with multiple sclerosis and his prognosis was uncertain. The environment of the clinic suited his ministry as the distances around the wards were considerably less than in many of the public hospitals, where travel about the hospital frequently involved walking considerable distances.

Multiple sclerosis is a condition that is totally unpredictable. It affects the musculoskeletal system and results in muscle weakness and disability. The severity and rate of progress waxes and wanes in a totally unpredictable fashion. I have vivid memories of Fr Gerry initially using a stick, subsequently crutches and, at times, spells in a wheelchair. The disability never limited his chaplaincy work. In truth, it had the opposite effect, in that he related to patients with such sincerity and understanding as he knew what it was to be in their position.

All patients, irrespective of their faith or creed, were treated with extraordinary compassion and understanding. I have fond memories of Fr Gerry telling me of the friendships he established with several Ulster unionists who attended Blackrock Clinic for cardiac surgery. The friendship and respect they shared was so sincere that many of these patients invited him to their homes in the North and he gladly accepted.

I write these few words with sincerity as I was the beneficiary of Fr Gerry's ministry at first hand when my late wife was a patient in the clinic for many months during the last year of her life on earth. Fr Gerry visited her almost every day. During this period, he was seriously ill himself and was a patient on another floor. This did not prevent his continuing with his priestly ministry. The comfort and solace that both my beloved wife and I received from his visits cannot be fully described or captured in words. During my wife's last twenty-four hours Fr Gerry visited her on three separate occasions. This was his unique quality.

Those of us who are involved in healthcare are motivated to care for the sick to the best of our ability. We are in a very privileged position. Patients entrust themselves to us with their most intimate problems and they entrust us surgeons with their lives. What other profession has such a privileged role? The older one becomes, the more one realises how limited our abilities are. With modern technology we can replaced diseased parts, insert stents to improve blood flow, transplant organs, combat various diseases with a multiplicity of drugs unimaginable a few decades ago. Yet how often, despite the advances and complexity of current care, are we powerless to influence the course of many outcomes? Medical science, despite all the advances, is still restricted in what can be achieved for the sick. What never changes, however, is the need to treat patients with the basic respect and dignity that is their due and that, for many, especially for those involved in chaplaincy, is informed and guided by the virtues of faith, hope and love.

In this increasingly secular age one might ask, 'Why the need for a hospital chaplain?' We've witnessed the numbers of those attending regular church services decimated in the Covid-19 pandemic. Even prior to this regular attendance at church services had been steadily falling and there is an increasing number of people who profess no religious belief. When patients are given a fatal diagnosis, despite their religious beliefs or practices in the past, many turn to the Lord for help and guidance. In these moments they welcome the hospital chaplain as he/she sits with them at this time, which is often initially characterised by darkness and despair.

Furthermore, and sadly, many professionals, despite their best efforts and sometimes due to a multiplicity of demands on their time, inadequate training and poor interpersonal skills, find it hard deliver the compassionate care that is needed by patients at particular points in time. Who remains to fill this void? In the past it was often the religious sisters who worked with the sick, aided by the hospital chaplain, who played an enormous role in caring for the spiritual needs of the patients. With the vast reduction in vocations to religious life the role of the hospital chaplain has become increasingly important. Working with other professionals, and as part of a multidisciplinary team, they continue to comfort and console both the sick and their relatives, and to bestow on them those virtues of faith, hope and love.

I had the privilege of visiting Fr Gerry a few weeks before he went to his eternal reward. He promised me he would give my darling wife a special hug from me as soon as they met. What more could I ask of his ministry? May his gentle soul rest in peace. I have no doubt he is with the Lord, and my own faith, hope and love help me to live with the belief that he continues his mission in caring for us all who were so privileged to know him.

Part Two

Perspectives of Hope

3: Could Chaplaincy Be an Instituted Ministry? A Study through the Lens of Hospital Chaplaincy

Eugene Duffy

'For Jesus the gravest sin, the kind that most effectively resists the reign of God, is the sin of causing suffering or remaining indifferent to it.'
José Pagola[1]

I have had two experiences of being attended to by chaplains while in hospital on two different occasions. I recall these because they alerted me to the strengths of this ministry and at the same time the pitfalls into which any one of us in ministry can, and do, so readily fall. The first one was a short stay for a routine procedure. An elderly priest chaplain visited me shortly after my admission. He spoke to me about my stay in the hospital; he was reassuring, easy and chatty in his manner. Towards the end of his visit, he said, 'Perhaps we can say a prayer together that all will be well for you.' There was a reassuring confidence in his approach, and I felt comforted by his visit. My second hospital experience of chaplaincy was quite different. This time it was for serious surgery. I had no visit from the chaplaincy before the operation. On the day following the surgery, Mass was broadcast on the internal TV facility, without sound! Then someone appeared unannounced in my room and asked if I would like to receive Communion. I put down my newspaper and said 'Yes'. I received Communion and, without any further comment, the chaplain was on his way. It could have been another tablet being dispensed. Later in the day, a trainee chaplain visited. The impression I got was that she was very nervous and was more conscious of her own

---

1   José Pagola, *Jesus: An Historical Approximation*, Miami, FL: Convivium Press, 2009.

behaviour than she was interested in me or my concerns. I mention these at the outset because they illustrate how sensitive a patient can be to the role a chaplain plays during a hospital stay. The more vulnerable patients are, the more acute their sensitivities; the more important the patient's own faith, the higher the expectations for that faith encounter with the chaplain.

These two memories serve as reminders that we can take our ministerial roles for granted and forget the uniqueness of each encounter. Moreover, hospital chaplaincy is a very valued ministry within the healthcare world. Once it was the preserve of clergy alone. Now the role is much more likely to be exercised by a lay person, and by members of other faith traditions. In this essay, I propose to focus on the role of the Catholic chaplain only, to situate it in the healing ministry of Christ and the Church and then suggest that this role be considered for recognition as an instituted ministry in the Church. Though the scope of this publication extends beyond the realm of the hospital, many of the themes of Jesus' ministry – loss, abandonment, isolation, neglect, guilt and sickness – can be applied to chaplaincy in its many forms and settings.

A Christological Basis for the Work of the Chaplain

When we look at the gospels, we see how central the healing ministry of Jesus was to his entire mission. Nearly forty per cent of the Gospel narratives are devoted to his healing activity. Traditionally the miracles of Jesus are classified as exorcisms, healings and nature miracles; of his thirty-one miracles, seventeen are in the healing category. Jesus was not simply curing physical ailments like blindness, deafness or leprosy. His approach was much more holistic. As Albert Nolan has noted, 'The healing effect of Jesus' preaching and teaching can hardly be exaggerated. In turning the world right side up he must have brought untold relief to those who felt overburdened and disadvantaged by the system of the time. With parables and sayings Jesus was trying to open the minds of his contemporaries to *see* the world differently, to *see* it as it really is – right side up – and above all to *see* God as our loving and forgiving Father, our *abba.*[2] His lifting of the burden of sin and guilt was central to his ministry, and this inevitably often led to the healing of other physical and psychological disorders.

The ministry of Jesus does not begin with any great reforming agenda; there is no ideological grandstanding. Jesus responds to the immediacy of the needs of those whom he encounters. St Mark presents the first day of Jesus' public life as predominantly one of curing various illnesses (Mark 1:21–45). José Pagola sketches what sickness in Galilee was like at the time.

> The sick people Jesus met suffered the afflictions one would
> expect in a poor and underdeveloped country: there were blind
> people, paralytics, deaf mutes, people with skin diseases, the
> mentally ill. Many were incurable, abandoned to their fate, and
> left without means of earning a living; they hobbled through
> life as beggars, constantly confronted with misery and hunger.
> Jesus saw them lying by the roadside, at the village entrance,
> or in the synagogues, pleading for pity from passers-by.[3]

In addition to the physical pain and stress that the sick in Galilee experienced, they also interpreted their situation very consciously in terms of their relationship with God, because for the Semitic mind health and sickness came from God. Sickness was seen as a punishment from God, either for one's own sins or the sins of one's kin (John 9:2). In consequence, one who was visited by God's wrath could then be excluded from the community, so that illness had physical, social and theological implications for all concerned. The sick were the most marginalised people whom Jesus encountered and it is to them that he reaches out above all others.

A number of the features of Jesus' response to the sick are worthy of attention. His healing ministry was central to his proclamation of the

---

2   Albert Nolan, *Jesus Today: A Spirituality of Radical Freedom*, Maryknoll, NY: Orbis Books, 2006, 78.
3   José Pagola, op. cit., 158.

Kingdom of God, thus giving people an experience of a new relationship with God. In restoring health to the sick, he gave his contemporaries a sign of the world that God wanted for everyone. His approach was simple, unlike other healers who used all kinds of charms, incantations and secret formulae to effect their cures; he relied on the healing love of God. He mediated this love by talking to those who were afflicted, by physically touching or laying hands on them. Those gestures embodied and sealed a relationship between him and those who were sick. That physical presence and human touch were in themselves reassuring and comforting.

Indeed, it is a hazard of contemporary medicine that it will neglect the importance of the spontaneous conversation and the healing hand that creates a certain bond of trust and reassurance between the medical personnel and the patient. There is the danger that the diagnosis and response to the sick person's condition will all happen around a computer screen and without the precious time spent physically with the patient. In this context, the role of the chaplain can be an invaluable complement to the vital work of the medical team. The chaplain can be a genuine sacramental expression of the reassuring reality of God's love for the patient.

There was a remarkable freedom and graciousness to the healing work of Jesus. He healed those who sought his help and demanded nothing in return. He never asked those whom he healed to join his band of disciples, nor did he link his cures to a moral reform agenda on the part of those whom he cured. He simply sent them on their way, to be reintegrated into their families and neighbourhoods. His healing ministry was not about winning adherents or making conversions. So, too, for contemporary hospital chaplains, their role is not to proselytise or to effect conversions. It is simply to mediate the unconditional love of God for all with whom they come in contact, irrespective of their physical or moral situations. As Pagola remarks, 'For Jesus the gravest sin, the kind that most effectively resists the reign of God, is the sin of causing suffering or remaining

27

indifferent to it.'[4] Those who attend to the care of the sick, in whatever capacity, whether consciously or not, are participating in the in-breaking of God's Kingdom here and now.

Continuing the Mission of Jesus

The mission of the early community of disciples is launched after the Pentecost event with a healing ministry. In Acts 3:1–10 Peter and John make their first public appearance by curing a man disabled from birth; later Peter cures Aeneas at Lydda (9:32–35), raises Dorcas from the dead (9:36–42) and cures a disabled person in Lycaonia (14:8–10).

Rodney Stark has shown convincingly how the remarkable charity of Christians during times of plague and major epidemics in the early centuries of the Church's existence added to the credibility of the Church and in consequence attracted numerous converts. Due to the charitable efforts of Christians, in imitation of the example of Jesus, their own survival rates and those of communities to whom they were able to reach out far surpassed those of the wider population, contributing to the spread of Christianity in the Empire.[5]

Dionysius, the bishop of Alexandria, has this to say in an Easter homily preached during a devastating plague in 260:

> Most of our fellow Christians showed unbounded love and loy-
> alty, never sparing themselves and thinking only of one anoth-
> er. Heedless of danger, they took charge of the sick, attending
> to their every need and ministering to them in Christ, and with
> them departed this life serenely happy; for they were infected
> by others with the disease, drawing on themselves the sick-
> ness of their neighbours and cheerfully accepting their pains.
> Many, in nursing and curing others, transferred their death to
> themselves and died in their stead. The best of our brothers and
> sister lost their lives in this manner, a number of presbyters,

4   Ibid., 17
5   See Chapter 4, 'Epidemics, Networks and Conversion', in Rodney Stark, *The Rise of Chris-
    tianity*, San Francisco, CA: HarperCollins, 1997, 73–94.

28

deacons, and laymen and women winning high commendation so that death in this form, the result of great piety and strong faith, seems in every way the equal of martyrdom.[6]

The care of the sick has remained a constant concern of the Church and, together with education, has made a significant contribution to human well-being. Throughout the Middle Ages, the care of the sick was an important outreach of monastic communities to their local hinterlands. Charlemagne decreed that each monastery and cathedral should have a hospital attached. These hospitals offered care to all, irrespective of their social class or religious affiliation. From the late ninth century, various confraternities and religious orders were established specifically to care for the sick. From the earliest period of the Church's presence in Ireland, care of the sick was an important aspect of its mission, as evidenced in place names like Hospital, Spittle, Ballinspittle, Spiddal, Leopardstown. From the nineteenth century the foundation of religious orders of women in Ireland show how central the care of the sick remained for the mission of the Church. Indeed, the work of the sisters had become so professional that the state was willing to cede responsibility for running most of the hospitals to them. Today the Church is the largest single provider of healthcare services in the world, estimated at providing twenty-six per cent of these facilities globally, and most significantly in the developing countries.[7]

Ecclesiological Grounding for Chaplaincy

The role of a Catholic chaplain, whether in a hospital, school, prison or any other institution, is one that represents the Christian community to which she or he belongs, even though very often the employer and paymaster may be a state or one of its organs. Despite the fact that the chaplain is often operating in an oasis within a secular world, one has still

6   Eusebius, *The History of the Church*, trans. G. A. Williamson, London: Penguin, 1965, 305, cited in Timothy Radcliffe, *Alive in God: A Christian Imagination*, London: Bloomsbury, 2019, 63–64.

7   'Catholic hospitals comprise one quarter of world's healthcare, council reports', Catholic News Agency, 10/02/2010, https://www.catholicnewsagency.com/news/18624/catholic-hospitals-comprise-one-quarter-of-worlds-healthcare-council-reports (accessed 10 July 2021).

to consider the ecclesial dimension of the chaplain's ministry, whether the chaplain is an ordained minister or not. For the Catholic chaplain, his or her ministry has to be grounded in the nature and mission of the Church itself. Indeed, how one understands the Church and its role will condition not only the content but also the style of that ministry. Forty years ago, the great German theologian Karl Rahner, in a way that was uncannily prescient of the vision of Pope Francis, said that the Church of the future 'should be thoroughly missionary'.[8]

We may recall that the Second Vatican Council, in its *Dogmatic Constitution on the Church,* described the Church 'as a sacrament or instrumental sign of intimate union with God and of the unity of all humanity', its purpose 'to raise human beings to share in the divine life'. We are reminded here that the Church is an effective sign of God's universal love for all peoples, but at the same time it is only a sign, because God's love extends and works far beyond the confines of the Church and her members. The sign is not identical with what is being signified, namely God's unconditional love for all. The Church and her members, who try to witness daily to that love made known in the life, death and resurrection of Christ, are beacons within a world that might otherwise be oblivious of the divine plan, which is to lead the entire family into the full embrace of the Father, Son and Holy Spirit.

This sacramental sign has an inner and an outer aspect. The inner aspect is God's universal, salvific love, ever active and dynamic. The outer aspect can be described using various metaphors or images, such as the people of God, the Body of Christ and, most recently by Pope Francis, 'the missionary community of the disciples of Jesus'. The image of discipleship suggests a community of people who are like apprentices, listening to and observing Jesus, learning from him as from a gentle mentor and being guided in their practice of 'the trade'. It is a humble and empowering image when compared with images such as 'the perfect

---

8   'The Future of Christian Communities', in *Theological Investigations XXI*, London: Darton, Longman & Todd, 1991, 122.

30

society', that were operative for so long, leading to authoritarian and clericalist mentalities, with all of their resultant problems. The missionary qualifier charges the community with a responsibility to give public witness to their faith in Christ, so that others seeing them and the joy that they experience will be attracted to their way of life and, ultimately, to enter into a relationship with Christ. Being a disciple is a learning adventure and too often, we shirk the adventure for safer, familiar havens that lack inspiration or challenge. Without the challenge of an adventure our faith, our community of disciples, will cease to be attractive to those outside its boundaries.

While we know that God's love is quietly at work in hidden ways, it remains part of the divine plan that this love be expressed and articulated in tangible and visible ways within the world. Those who have encountered the love of God in the person of Christ under the influence of the Holy Spirit are impelled and obliged to share this with others, in whatever ways they can. This may be in the silent, attentive and patient presence of a chaplain or carer sitting by the bedside of a seriously ill patient, just as much as in the sermon of an eloquent preacher at the lectern.

While we have traditionally emphasised the 'ontological change' that occurs in the case of an ordained minister, we overlook the far more fundamental ontological change that occurs in baptism, when one is put in a fundamentally new and permanent relationship with Christ. It is this baptismal call that is of primary significance. For those, then, who are formed in the faith and practice of the life of discipleship, there is an urgency and an imperative to give expression to this in their lives. The missionary impulse is part of the baptised condition because the gifts of faith and grace received in baptism are meant to be shared and used in building up the missionary community of disciples.

Vocational Nature of Chaplaincy

Recent research among a representative group of hospital chaplains has shown that they regard their work as vocational, many seeing it as a faith response to their search for meaning and fulfilment in their lives.[9] The decision to pursue a ministry in chaplaincy appears as a process of discernment, arising from the ordinary encounters and concerns that life puts one's way, but very often in the context of suffering and loss. This points to a reflectiveness in living, which is a mark of mature discipleship. It would seem that most of those who become involved in hospital chaplaincy do so following an earlier career option, which again points to the fact that they have life experiences and maturity that may not always be the case in other ministerial positions. In the narratives that people presented, the elements of a true vocation were obvious, including a sense of being called by God, the possession of important attributes like empathy, listening skills, being vulnerable with others, a non-judgemental disposition, a willingness to learn from experience, and reassurance and confirmation by friends and co-workers. Among some, there was the recognition of the contribution that spiritual care can make to the personal healing of a patient. All of these traits are consistent with those required of a mature Christian disciple who is taking the faith journey seriously and responding to the promptings of the Spirit at work in them. They are also indicative of how nature and grace work harmoniously in those who are open to the divine action in their lives. Chaplains are professional carers to the sick, while at the same time being ministers of Christ's compassion towards his people.

Most chaplains see their work as providing a caring, empathetic presence for those who are experiencing some significant transition in their lives. They see themselves as providing an attentive presence to those who are vulnerable, attempting to make sense of suffering, pain or loss. For those who are disposed to a faith perspective, they see themselves as supporting patients in finding God in their situations and all of them found that their own faith provided them with a scaffolding to sustain them in their ministry.

9 Margaret Naughton, 'Standing in the Gap: A Theological Reflection on The Meaning, Value and Significance of Faith in The Life and Ministry of Healthcare Chaplains', unpublished PhD thesis submitted to Mary Immaculate College, University of Limerick, 2021.

These perspectives offered by chaplains in that recent study echo something of the message of Pope Paul VI to the sick at the conclusion of the Second Vatican Council:

> But we have something deeper and more valuable to give you, the only truth capable of answering the mystery of suffering and of bringing you relief without illusion, and that is faith and union with the Man of Sorrows, with Christ the Son of God, nailed to the cross for our sins and for our salvation. Christ did not do away with suffering. He did not even wish to unveil to us entirely the mystery of suffering. He took suffering upon Himself and this is enough to make you understand all its value. All of you who feel heavily the weight of the cross, you who are poor and abandoned, you who weep, you who are persecuted for justice, you who are ignored, you the unknown victims of suffering, take courage. You are the preferred children of the kingdom of God, the kingdom of hope, happiness and life. You are the brothers of the suffering Christ, and with Him, if you wish, you are saving the world.

> This is the Christian science of suffering, the only one which gives peace. Know that you are not alone, separated, abandoned or useless. You have been called by Christ and are His living and transparent image. In His name, the council salutes you lovingly, thanks you, assures you of the friendship and assistance of the Church, and blesses you.[10]

His words addressed to the sick resonate with those who work as chaplains in healthcare contexts. Theirs is not a medical role but it is nonetheless important in providing for the holistic care of the sick. The chaplain may provide very ordinary human services for the sick but in these gestures can communicate in a tangible way the love of God at work among God's people. Pope Francis spoke of the key role played by

---

10   Pope Paul VI, 'Address of Pope Paul VI to the poor, the sick and the suffering', 8 December 1965, https://www.vatican.va/content/paul-vi/en/speeches/1965/documents/hf_p-vi_spe_19651208_epilogo-concilio-poveri.html.

chaplains in an address to healthcare workers following the devastation wrought by the Covid-19 pandemic in Lombardy:

> Patients often felt they had 'angels' at their side, who helped them recover their health and, at the same time, comforted, supported, and at times accompanied them to the threshold of the final encounter with the Lord. These healthcare workers, sustained by the concern of hospital chaplains, witnessed God's closeness to those who suffer; they were silent artisans of the culture of closeness and tenderness. And you were its witnesses, even in the little things: in the caresses … , even with cell phones, you connected elderly persons who were about to die, with their son, with their daughter, to say goodbye to them, to see them for the last time … ; small gestures of the creativity of love … . This was good for all of us. The witness of closeness and tenderness.[11]

Chaplaincy as Ministry

Traditionally, chaplaincy was a role exercised by ordained priests and generally associated with sacramental services, celebrating the Eucharist, hearing confessions and administering the sacrament of the sick. Today, priest chaplains are in a minority and the greater part of the ministry is less in the sacramental dimension and more in the caring and spiritual dimensions. Obviously, the sacramental aspect is still important and the sacrament of the sick has a prominent role in the chaplaincy service. The role of hospital chaplain then juxtaposes two forms of ministry. Some chaplains are ordained and others work on the basis of the common priesthood of the baptised, thus both provide services that often overlap and at other times do not.

The Second Vatican Council helped to articulate formally the various ways in which all of the baptised members of the Church share in its

---

11 Pope Francis, 'Address of His Holiness Pope Francis to the Doctors, Nurses and Healthcare Workers from the Lombardy', Saturday 20 June 2020, https://www.vatican.va/content/francesco/en/speeches/2020/june/documents/papa-francesco_20200620_operatorisanitari-lombardia.html.

mission of proclaiming the Kingdom of God. The ecclesiology of communion, which underpinned the conciliar thinking, highlighted again the complementarity of gifts that enrich the Church for mission. It acknowledged that the Holy Spirit is the source of this variety of gifts building up the Church. Before the council, 'ministry' had a narrow meaning and was confined almost exclusively to those who were ordained. Although the word 'ministry' occurs about 200 times in the conciliar documents, there is an element of ambiguity about the basis for it. In some cases, 'ministry is seen as a sharing in the ministry or works of the ordained; in others it arises from the common priesthood' (*Lumen Gentium*, 10). But in its final document the council applied the word 'ministry' to ordinary activities of human life: earthly service (*Gaudium et Spes*, 38); safeguarding life (*Gaudium et Spes*, 51); service of security and liberty by soldiers (*Gaudium et Spes*, 79).[12] The post-synodal exhortation *Christifideles Laici* uses three terms: 'ministries', 'offices' and 'roles'. However, it is anxious to distinguish between the ministries that derive from ordination and those that derive from baptism:

> The ordained ministries, apart from the persons who receive them, are a grace for the entire Church. These ministries express and realise a participation in the priesthood of Jesus Christ that is different, not simply in degree but in essence, from the participation given to all the lay faithful through Baptism and Confirmation. On the other hand, the ministerial priesthood, as the Second Vatican Council recalls, essentially has the royal priesthood of all the faithful as its aim and is ordered to it.[13]

The exhortation then goes on to outline the conditions in which the faithful might exercise their ministry in virtue of their baptism and confirmation:

> When necessity and expediency in the Church require it, the

12 Christopher O'Donnell, *Ecclesia: A Theological Encyclopedia of the Church,* Collegeville, MN: Liturgical Press, 1996, s.v. Ministry.
13 *Christifideles Laici,* 22.

Pastors, according to established norms from universal law, can entrust to the lay faithful certain offices and roles that are connected to their pastoral ministry but do not require the character of Orders. The Code of Canon Law states: ' When the necessity of the Church warrants it and when ministers are lacking, lay persons, even if they are not lectors or acolytes, can also supply for certain of their offices, namely, to exercise the ministry of the word, to preside over liturgical prayers, to confer Baptism, and to distribute Holy Communion in accord with the prescriptions of the law' [can 230 §2]. However, *the exercise of such tasks does not make Pastors of the lay faithful:* in fact, a person is not a minister simply in performing a task, but through sacramental ordination. Only the Sacrament of Orders gives the ordained minister a particular participation in the office of Christ, the Shepherd and Head, and in his Eternal Priesthood [*Presbyterorum Ordinis*, 2 and 5]. The task exercised in virtue of supply takes its legitimacy formally and immediately from the official deputation given by the Pastors, as well as from its concrete exercise under the guidance of ecclesiastical authority.[14]

Here it can be seen that there is a certain reserve about applying the word ministry to those offices, roles and tasks that are not derived from ordination.

In his first apostolic exhortation, *Evangelii Gaudium,* Pope Francis spoke with a sense of urgency of the need to adapt ecclesial structures to better equip them for mission and evangelisation. He said:

The renewal of structures demanded by pastoral conversion can only be understood in this light: as part of an effort to make them more mission-oriented, to make ordinary pastoral activity on every level more inclusive and open, to inspire in pastoral workers a constant desire to go forth and in this way to

14   Ibid., 23.

elicit a positive response from all those whom Jesus summons to friendship with himself (27).[15]

Similarly, in his post-synodal exhortation, *Querida Amazonia*, he makes a plea for more lay ministries and 'mature and lay leaders endowed with authority'. He acknowledges that 'wherever there is a particular need, [the Holy Spirit] has already poured out the charisms that can meet it. This requires the Church to be open to the Spirit's boldness, to trust in, and concretely permit, the growth of a specific ecclesial culture that is *distinctively* lay' (94).[16]

In the meantime, Pope Francis has issued two documents on ministries that belong to the baptised faithful; both show a more expansive approach to the use of the word 'ministry', while at the same time retaining the distinction between the common and the ordained priesthood. These documents also demonstrate his own commitment to expanding and strengthening the position of lay ministries in the Church.

In his 'Letter to the Prefect of the Congregation for the Doctrine of the Faith, regarding access of women to the ministries of lector and acolyte', he offered a helpful clarification with regard to the nature and extent of ministry:

> … the Apostle Paul distinguishes between gifts of grace – charisms ('charismata') and services ('diakoniai' – 'minsteria' [cf. Rom 12:4ff and 1 Cor 12:12ff]). According to the tradition of the Church the diverse forms that charisms assume when they are publicly recognised and are made available to the community and to its mission in stable form are called ministries.
>
> In some cases a ministry has its origin in a specific sacrament, the Sacred Order: it pertains to the 'ordained' ministries, of the bishop, the priest, the deacon. In other cases the ministry

15 Pope Francis, *Evangelii Gaudium*, https://www.vatican.va/content/francesco/en/apost_exhortations/documents/papa-francesco_esortazione-ap_20131124_evangelii-gaudium.pdf.
16 Pope Francis, *Querida Amazonia*, https://www.vatican.va/content/francesco/en/apost_exhortations/documents/papa-francesco_esortazione-ap_20200202_querida-amazonia.html.

is entrusted, with a liturgical act of the bishop, to a person who has received Baptism and Confirmation and in whom specific charisms are recognised, after an appropriate journey of preparation: we then speak of 'instituted' ministries. Many other ecclesial services or offices are in fact exercised by many members of the community, for the good of the Church, often for a long period and with great efficacy, without the expectation of a particular rite for the bestowal of the role.[17]

In his most recent apostolic letter, *Antiquum ministerium*, he once again reiterates the need for an expansion of lay ministries in the Church:

> Awakening personal enthusiasm on the part of all the baptized and reviving the awareness of their call to carry out a proper mission in the community demands attentiveness to the voice of the Spirit, who is unfailingly present and fruitful (cf. CIC can. 774 §1; CCEO can. 617). Today, too, the Spirit is calling men and women to set out and encounter all those who are waiting to discover the beauty, goodness, and truth of the Christian faith. It is the task of pastors to support them in this process and to enrich the life of the Christian community through the recognition of lay ministries capable of contributing to the transformation of society through the 'penetration of Christian values into the social, political and economic sectors' (*Evangelii Gaudium*, 102, #5).[18]

The direction in which Pope Francis is pointing, then, begs the question as to whether healthcare chaplaincy should be designated as a specific ministry. It is evident from the response by chaplains to the questions in the survey already mentioned, that they see themselves as having a calling to this ministry. Obviously, some chaplains are already ordained

17 Pope Francis, 'Letter of His Holiness Pope Francis to the Prefect of the Congregation for the Doctrine of the Faith regarding Access of Women to the Ministries of Lector and Acolyte', https://www.vatican.va/content/francesco/en/letters/2021/documents/papa-frances-co_20210110_lettera-donne-lettorato-accolitato.pdf.
18 Pope Francis, *Antiquum Ministerium*, https://www.vatican.va/content/francesco/en/motu_proprio/documents/papa-francesco-motu-proprio-20210510_antiquum-ministerium.html.

ministers in the Church, which means that their ministry extends beyond the limits of the healthcare context. However, the significant number of lay chaplains warrants consideration in terms of how their roles are designated. The approach being taken by Pope Francis accords well with the widely accepted criteria for ministry as formerly proposed by T. F. O'Meara. According to O'Meara, 'Ministry is: (1) doing something; (2) for the advent of the Kingdom; (3) in public; (4) on behalf of a Christian community; (5) which is a gift received in faith, baptism and ordination; (6) which is an activity with its own limits and identity within a diversity of ministerial actions.'[19] In light of these criteria and the impetus given to lay ministry by Pope Francis, there appear to be good grounds for proposing that healthcare chaplaincy be considered an instituted ministry in the Church.

Ministry in the Church has been flexible throughout the course of history. As Peter Schmidt has pointed out, ecclesial 'structures must constantly seek new paradigms for realizing God's covenant will sacramentally, so that these can be signs of God's will in the world', and that will is 'opting uncompromisingly for human well-being'.[20] Schmidt goes on to argue that attention to the concept of time alerts us to the realisation that Church structures cannot be kept unchanged with a predetermined model all down the ages. He argues that for too long the Church has thought in a timeframe that characterised the early Church, a time when the eschaton was expected in the near future. Our time frames are now much longer and therefore those of the New Testament are no longer applicable in an uncritical fashion. He says, '[T]he mere possibility – and perhaps actuality – of a very long span of time (which means nothing cosmologically) now shows that forms and traditions, however venerable, are by definition relative and subject to evolution, because they are temporal. They *cannot* be absolute, and the

---

19 In Joseph Komonchak, Mary Collins and Dermot Lane, *The New Dictionary of Theology*, Dublin: Gill & Macmillan, 1987, s.v. Ministry.
20 'Ministries in the New Testament and Early Church', in Jan Kerkhofs, *Europe without Priests?* London: SCM Press, 1995, 46–47.

immutability of God's will cannot depend on the immutability of their historical form.'[21] On this basis, new forms of ministry have to develop in response to the needs of humankind as it moves through history with all of the inevitable change that brings.

While in some of the statements of Pope Francis there may be a reaffirmation of the sacraments being the preserve of the ordained ministers, there is at the same time an emphasis on ecclesial ministry that can be exercised by all of the baptised. There are some tensions in his position that cannot be addressed here. However, more recently, Hervé Legrand has drawn attention to the fact that until the systematisation of sacramental thought in the scholastic period, these distinctions between baptised and ordained were not as rigid as they then became. The entire community of the baptised was considered as the celebrant of the sacraments. Legrand suggests that the category of ministry is more helpful than speaking of two priesthoods (that of the baptised and that of the ordained), because for the greater part of the Church's history the emphasis has been on the Church as an assembly of the baptised conferring and celebrating the sacraments. He points out that for the fifteen hundred years preceding Trent almost all of the sacraments could be conferred by any of the baptised in case of necessity, including confession and the sacrament of the sick.[22] Surely there is an invitation here for further reflection on which sacraments may be conferred by lay chaplains.

Ministry in Overlapping Contexts

The focus throughout has been on the role of the Catholic chaplain in a healthcare context. This is not to overlook the fact that other denominations and faith traditions also provide chaplaincy services in healthcare facilities, often side by side with one another. Therefore, here we will only consider the issues confronting the Catholic chaplain. Apart from

---

21 Ibid., 50.
22 'Le pouvoir sacerdotal doit êtrecompris, selon la grand Tradition, comme un ministère de l'unique sacerdoce du Christ', in Michel Camessus, *Transformer L'Église: quelques propositions à la lumière de* Fratelli Tutti, Montrouge: Bayard Presse, 2020, 152.

40

acting from a faith motivation, the chaplain is generally the employee of a secular institution, either the state or a public hospital. Inevitably, the secular institution will have its own workplace standards, guidelines and expectations. It may demand certain qualifications or compliance with certain accreditation standards, just as the Church may set its own criteria for the role. These may not necessarily conflict with one another, except that the Catholic chaplain may require a mandate from her or his bishop. In the absence of such mandate, then the service provided, while it may be beneficial in its own right, could not be considered an ecclesial ministry.

In the current Irish context, there is greater diversity in religious practice and affiliation. This poses significant challenges for Catholic chaplains, since they can no longer presume that those whom they visit on their rounds will share their faith or practise it. They will encounter the devout Catholic, the non-practising, those of other faiths and atheists. Each of these presents its own challenges for the chaplain. The devout Catholic may expect to receive the sacraments as part of their pastoral care while ill, in which case an ordained minister will have to provide these. They may also expect that the chaplain will pray with them and for them in their pain or weakness, as well as providing an empathetic listening presence. With Christians of other denominations, similar prayer and presence may be greatly appreciated.

Ministering to those of other faiths or none can be more challenging, but is nonetheless a genuine exercise of ministry. Anyone who, in the name of Christ, provides comfort and support to a person in need is giving expression to the Kingdom of God and making it a concrete reality in the world, irrespective of how the recipient perceives the encounter. Such a genuinely human act is an extension of the Church's mission, even if the names of God or Christ are not invoked.

Although there is not a significant body of research about how chaplains, or other workers, negotiate religious difference in the workplace, there is some evidence to suggest that two main approaches are adopted by chaplains when they minister to those who do not share their own faith. The first is to 'neutralise', where they affirm or support the patient's particular religious tradition. They may also do this by emphasising the human and the spiritual dimensions of life, reflecting on shared human experiences rather than speaking of faith. Inevitably, these strategies can pose inner tensions for the chaplain, especially when dealing with issues of meaning and value, for example how to integrate suffering into one's life, or with issues that have significant moral dimensions, such as end-of-life issues.

A second method for negotiating these situation is 'code-switching', that is, 'they move between religious languages, symbols, and, sometimes rituals in their work with patients and families'.[23] For example, in speaking to a Muslim, the chaplain would speak of Allah or the Koran. However, if possible, chaplains will try to establish a link with the patient's own religious minister. It would seem that most chaplains are better prepared through clinical pastoral education to neutralise than to code-switch when dealing with inter-faith encounters.

Conclusion

While this essay has focused on the work of the healthcare chaplain, much of what has been said could apply to any chaplaincy role, in a school, a university, a prison, a military institution etc. The argument was being made that this work is a significant ministry in the Church and could be considered as an instituted ministry in due course and with expanded sacramental powers. To date, chaplaincy roles are confined to a relatively small number of social institutions, such as those mentioned above. Perhaps, given the recognised value of healthcare chaplaincy, the time has come for those in ecclesial leadership to think more broadly about this ministry. Might it not be a good idea to have chaplains to some of the very large financial and manufacturing sites that exist across the

---

23 Wendy Cadge and Emily Sigalow, 'Negotiating Religious Differences: The Strategies of Inter-faith Chaplains in Healthcare', in *Journal for the Scientific Study of Religion* 52 (2013), 153.

country? Are there not needs among workers on these sites that would be positively met with a well-resourced chaplaincy service? It may be the only opportunity that some of these workers may find to access an ecclesial minister in time of a relational breakdown, a bereavement or the prospect of becoming unemployed. These are basic human experiences that call for support, for someone to accompany those affected so that they can find meaning and direction in their crises. It may be that 'on site' is the only likelihood of them encountering a person of faith who can provide that important element of support. The healthcare chaplaincy already provides a model from which to learn.

4: The History of Chaplaincy Down The Ages

Ciarán O'Carroll

'Lord, if your people still need me,
I do not refuse the work.
Thy will be done.'
St Martin of Tours

Beginnings

The history of chaplaincy, in the widest sense of the term, dates from the era of the Roman Empire.[1] Constantine was the first Roman emperor to convert to Christianity. It is said that this occurred following a divine personal revelation on the eve of the Battle of the Milvean Bridge in October 312. Constantine's victory in battle later gained him independent and absolute power over the Roman Empire. Eusebius of Caesarea and Lactantius, two important Roman historians, describe how an extraordinary vision, immediately prior to the battle, convinced Constantine to fight under the protection of the Christian God. Constantine's vision marked the beginning of his journey of conversion to Christianity. He favoured the Christian Church from the time of this battle, and was baptised towards the end of his life. Constantine is now popularly referenced as the 'First Christian Emperor'.

During Constantine's reign, Christianity began its evolution from a persecuted religion towards a position where it was effectively the dominant faith of the Roman Empire. In a reference to Constantine, Eusebius recorded:

When he engaged in a war he caused a tent to be borne before

[1]   See Doris L. Bergen, *The Sword of the Lord, Military Chaplains from the First to the Twenty-First Century*, Notre Dame, IN: University of Notre Dame Press, 2004.

44

him, constructed in the shape of a church, so that in case he or his army might be led into the desert, they might have a sacred edifice in which to praise and worship God and participate in the mysteries. Priests and deacons followed the tent, who fulfilled the orders about these matters, according to the law of the church.[2]

The accuracy of this unique account of Christian clergy accompanying Roman armies in the fourth century is disputed by some historians, but there are sporadic but ample validated references to the appointment of Christian priests to Roman army units by the middle of the fifth century.

Constantine is viewed as the first baptised emperor who recognised that, in the face of the ambiguities of human existence, the Christian religion can give meaning to the secular world in which people live, can confer unity on diverse groups of citizens and inspire allegiance in otherwise divided groups of tribes and families, nations and states. This understanding of the potentially key unifying role of religious belief was embraced by successive generations of emperors, political rulers and royal families in the centuries that followed.

The Early Centuries AD

During the later years of the Roman Empire, Christian clerics accompanied armies in the field. During the fourth and fifth centuries the profession of the Christian faith and the renunciation of a sinful past had significant consequences for military personnel. Once a soldier had converted to Christianity or confessed his past sins and received penance he was mandated to retire from military life. In the fifth century Pope Leo I stated, in a letter to Bishop Rusticus of Narbonne, that 'it is completely contrary to all the rules of the church for a soldier to return to duty after receiving penance'.[3] Later, under the influence of Irish missionaries in the seventh century, the old system of 'once in a lifetime' penance evolved to the

---

2   See *Life of Constantine the Great* by Eusebius of Caesarea, 4.18—9: Nicene and post Nicene Fathers, 1:544–45.

3   Pope Leo I, *Epistolae*, PL 54:1206–7.

practice of repeatable penance. With the development of 'penitentials', a series of Church rules or guidelines on the subject of the sacrament of penance began to circulate in the Christian world. The penitentials, which effectively prescribed penances in the confessional, were first developed by Celtic monks in Ireland in the sixth century. They consisted of a list of sins and the appropriate penances prescribed for them, and were employed as a type of manual for confession. This development in Christian doctrine underscored the requirement for, and the influence of, chaplains. Their number and ministry expanded in the service of Christian troops as it became necessary to provide large numbers of soldiers with the opportunity to confess their sins before they went into battle. Every unit commander was expected to have a dedicated chaplain responsible for the celebration of the sacrament and the assignment of penances to soldiers.

St Martin of Tours

Martin of Tours is the saint synonymous with early Christian chaplaincy. The medieval accounts of his life describe this compassionate, fourth-century soldier who converted to Christianity after he encountered a half-naked, shivering homeless man on a cold winter's night at the gate of the city of Amiens, in northern France. Having no money in his purse, this soldier took off his cloak and slashed it with his sword in order to share it with the homeless man. Later that night the same homeless man appeared to the soldier in a dream, wearing the half-cloak, and revealed himself to be Jesus Christ. As a result of this experience, this soldier, destined to become St Martin of Tours, converted to Christianity and was baptised.

Capella

The relic of the remaining half of his cloak grew to become central to the cult of St Martin. It was deemed to be so important that successive members of the Frankish royalty had a representation of the torn cloak imprinted on a royal banner to signify 'the presence of God' in war. Sacred oaths were frequently sworn upon it. The Franks brought this *cappa* of St Martin with them into battles in the belief that it would enhance their chances of attaining victory. As early as the fourth century, the structure in which the half-cloak was preserved was referred to as a *cappella* (diminutive of *cappa*), a term that came to be used widely for buildings that served to keep relics and from which the modern word 'chapel' as a place of worship is derived. Since the *cappella* was a sacred relic of the Church, a priest accompanied it as a custodian. These clerics carried and cared for the *cappa* of St Martin.[4]

Charlemagne

Initially this sacred relic gave its name to the tent, and later to the simple oratory, or chapel, where it was preserved. Other relics were added later and these were guarded by chaplains appointed by the king during the Merovingian and Carolingian periods. This practice was particularly prominent during the reign of Charlemagne, who appointed clerical ministers *(cappellani)* who lived in the royal palace. These chaplains attended to the king's religious needs. Their primary duty was the safekeeping of the sacred relics, but they also celebrated Mass for the king on feast days, worked in conjunction with the royal notaries and wrote any documents requested by the king. The duties of chaplains thus gradually evolved towards direct service to the monarch, acting as advisers in both ecclesiastical and secular matters.

This practice of kings personally appointing their chaplains became widespread throughout western Christendom. Many of the royal chaplains were appointed to bishoprics and the highest offices in the Church. In time, the tradition of military chaplains providing pastoral care across Europe and the eastern Mediterranean became established from the early Middle Ages onwards. In 742, the Frankish government

4   The account of St Martin's cloak was first recorded in the *Vita sancti Martini (Life of St Martin)* of Sulpicius Severus (363–c. 425). This work survives in a number of medieval copies, such as the twelfth-century manuscripts Cotton MS Tiberius D IV/1 and Harley MS 4984, both possibly originating from England.

formally established the office of unit chaplain, whose duties included hearing confession and assigning penances to those soldiers in his care. In medieval Europe, chaplains were assigned to prepare and accompany troops, and presumably to support the soldiers through the daily terrors inherent in warfare. This practice has remained in place since that time and is part of modern military life.

There is evidence that both Pope Hadrian I in the eighth century and Emperor Charlemagne shared concerns regarding the pastoral care of members of the military. Charlemagne recorded that during the early part of the campaign against the Avars in 791, three days of litanies, led by the priests, were observed from 5 to 7 September. Everyone in the camp participated. God's mercy was implored and his aid sought. The prayers specifically requested that God would grant them victory in battle and keep them safe from danger. Each priest celebrated a special Mass and every cleric sang fifty psalms.

'God Wills It'

As combat loomed, early medieval chaplains sought to maintain the morale of the fighters and exercised pastoral care as fears of imminent death preoccupied the soldiers. Homilies preached from the late eighth century urged every soldier to take advantage of the opportunities given to them through the presence of a chaplain to confess their sins prior to battle. There are numerous accounts of how chaplains led liturgical services and special votive Masses prior to battle. There are several reports of Carolingian warriors, and later the Crusaders, fasting for days before battle to purify themselves, feasting only on the Eucharist. The blessing of the standards, or the related custom of following a processional cross or a prized relic, such as the Crusades' 'Holy Lance', became established customs. At the time of the Crusades, the rallying cry of 'God wills it' unified the troops as they prepared for battle. Liturgies accompanying the burial of the fallen following battle, or services of thanksgiving in victory, were invariably led by chaplains. The organisation and the celebration of annual commemorative services for the fallen, presided over by chaplains, gradually became a frequently recorded feature in medieval Europe.

The Chaplain's Duties

In the early years of the ninth century, Benedict the Levite, also known as 'Benedict Levita of Mainz', or 'Benedict the Deacon', compiled a controversial collection of mostly forged edicts in which he detailed the obligations and tasks of a chaplain while serving with military forces on campaign. This author presented his collection as the continuation and completion of the collection of genuine capitularies in four books, *Capitularia Regum Francorum*, attributed in 827 to Ansegisus, Abbot of Fontenelle. These documents provide a list of the military chaplain's duties. They also include a detailed description of the essential role of chaplaincy for the war effort. The author outlined that clerics were obliged to celebrate Mass and to beseech God's aid with the aim of securing victory in battle. Chaplains were deputed to recite litanies, give charitable donations and pray to God on behalf of the army. Benedict noted the explicit role of the chaplain in the provision of pastoral care to the troops.

Several historians provide evidence that prelates acted as chaplains towards the end of the first millennium. An account by Gerhard, the provost of St Mary's Cathedral in Augsburg, describes the pastoral actions of Bishop Ulrich of Augsburg during a siege of the city by a Hungarian army in 955. The account emphasised how Bishop Ulrich reassured his troops that by honouring Christ, protections would be afforded to many, and he underlined how the Psalms offered the prospect of God's mercy for the living, and eternal rest for those who died. It was Gerhard's opinion that this homily inspired the men to stand and fight in the face of any odds.

Spiritual Preparation

The importance of spiritual preparation for soldiers who were preparing for war was consistently highlighted in the late tenth and early eleventh centuries, in a military struggle between German forces and the Slavs. As a new millennium dawned, the obligation for all chaplains to provide spiritual support to their troops was highlighted. In the opening years of the new millennium, Bishop Burchard of Worms, a noted canonist, drafted a handbook or manual for bishops in which he detailed the sacramental and moral duties of chaplains. Some decades later, Bishop Ivo of Chartres detailed the canonical, moral and sacramental responsibilities of military chaplains. He noted that military chaplains were neither to carry arms nor to engage in battle. Instead, they were required to celebrate Mass for the military forces in the field and to hear confessions. Furthermore, chaplains were obliged to provide spiritual care to the wounded and dying both during and following conflicts.

The English historian William of Malmesbury (c.1090–c.1143) described the Battle of Hastings, which took place in 1066, and the effect of the battle on England. It was a battle between Anglo-Saxon King Harold II and the Norman-French army of William, the Duke of Normandy, popularly known as William the Conqueror. As a result of Harold's death in battle, William became King William I of England. William of Malmesbury recorded how chaplains celebrated the sacrament of confession with the troops of William the Conqueror prior to battle. This was contrasted with the behaviour of Harold's troops, who allegedly indulged in drunken revelry. On the morning of the battle it was noted that even Duke William himself participated in the celebration of the Eucharist.[5]

Robert Wace, popularly referred to as Wace, was the twelfth-century medieval Norman poet and historian of the Norman conquest by King Henry II of England (1154–1189). He described how clerics fulfilled their duties as they heard the confessions of the Norman troops, assigned

5   William of Malmesbury, *Gesta Regum Anglorum*, Marjorie Chibnall (ed.), Oxford: Oxford University Press, 1998, 2:454.

penances and granted the men absolution. Priests were also recorded as having offered prayers on behalf of the soldiers. Wace wrote that on the eve of the battle, while the troops slept, chaplains organised prayer vigils, reciting psalms and chanting litanies. With the outbreak of battle, they continued to pray for victory. Chaplains to the Anglo-Norman army blessed the troops with relics and crosses and ensured that religious banners were visible in the field.[6]

Fourth Lateran Council

In the thirteenth century, during the reign of Pope Innocent III (1198–1216), the nature of the office of military chaplains was described in the context of the Fourth Lateran Council. This council, the largest and most representative of the medieval councils to that date, was the most significant papal assembly of the later Middle Ages. The council was convoked by Pope Innocent III with the papal bull *Vineam Domini Sabaoth* of 19 April 1215, and it was convened at Rome's Lateran Palace on 11 November 1215. The last decree of the council dealt with preparations for a crusade and fixed a date for its commencement, later reviewed due to the death of the pontiff. In the final canon, Pope Innocent enunciated the responsibilities of military chaplains in the context of a crusade. The papal document *Ad liberandum* authorised the recruitment of priests and bishops to serve with the army for a set period of time, ensuring a continuity of pastoral care over the entire course of the campaign. The moral obligation of chaplains, as outlined by the pontiff, were twofold: to exhort the soldiers to behave properly as Christians and to teach the troops by example to maintain a proper spirit of Christian fear of the Lord.[7]

Military chaplains went on to play critical roles in recruitment, ministry and participation in Crusader armies. On the day prior to the first major assault by the Latin Crusaders against Constantinople on 5 July 1203, a chaplain to the forces, Henry of Valenciennes, recorded how

---

6   See Wace, *Le Roman de Rou*, A. J. Holden (ed.), Paris: A. & J. Picard, 1971, 2:157.
7   See *Conciliorum Oecumenicorum Decreta,* 3rd ed., Bologna: Istituto per le Scienze Religiose, 1973, 267.

chaplains, both bishops and priests, addressed the army, emphasising the importance of each man confessing his sins prior to combat.[8]

Conflictual

By the middle of the thirteenth century, the sacramental and moral aspects of the chaplain's office were legally established in law.[9] On 9 August 1238, in a papal bull issued to the Franciscan and Dominican order, Pope Gregory IX (1227–41) outlined a detailed list of the duties and responsibilities of every military chaplain in the Hungarian royal army, which was preparing for a military campaign against the Bulgarians. It was emphasised that chaplains were there to celebrate the sacraments and the pontiff authorised chaplains to grant the troops remission of their sins. In addition to their sacramental responsibilities, chaplains were ordered to provide moral encouragement to the troops in their homilies.[10]

The chaplaincy role carried inherent contradictions of function within the military organisation. The chaplain was a religious figure who symbolised the tension between the vision of a Church that preached the importance of peace and reconciliation, mercy and forgiveness, on the one hand, and, on the other, the expectations of a state regarding a soldier's responsibilities in wartime to fight and defend his country or cause to the death, when deemed necessary. The incorporation of a blessing of the actions of one's government into the duties of the chaplain indicated their ambiguous role within the military.

The role of religion as an influential factor in the sustenance and support of armies and their fighting spirit is challenging to analyse. There exists a plausible correlation between religion and patriotism, yet there is an inherent contradiction between some of the causes fought throughout the ages and the central message of the Gospel.

8   See Geoffroi de Villehardouin, *La conquête de Constantinople*, 1:152, and Henri de Valen-
     ciennes, *Histoire de l'Empereur Henri de Constantinople*, 7–8.
9   See 'The Friars Go to War: Mendicant Military Chaplains, 1216–c. 1300', David S.
     Bachrach in *The Catholic Historical Review*, Vol. 90, No. 4 (October 2004), 617–33.
10 See Christoph T. Maier, *Preaching the Crusades: Mendicant Friars and the Cross in the
     Thirteenth Century*, New York, NY: Cambridge University Press, 1994, 177ff.

Moral Purpose

Again and again, there were chaplains ministering to armies on both sides of a conflict. This has been especially well documented from the time of the Reformation to the present day. As in previous generations, several chaplains became famous for their preaching, frequently confirming the special place held by that army in God's eyes. The substance of the chaplain's political message derived from the idea that God had chosen one army – the one for which they fought![11] This proclamation of one-sided political messages meant that military chaplains down the ages were repeatedly confronted with complicated theological questions that had far-reaching consequences.

Spiritual ministry is challenging for those whose are tasked with fighting for their country or particular cause, and who, if the need arises, are called upon to kill others and put their own lives at risk. Successive generations of military chaplains were required to interpret the fifth commandment in a way that would not burden the souls of soldiers for whom their Christian faith was important. Chaplains have counselled believers, and those in their charge , 'how to suffer, how to make of physical pain, personal loss, worldly defeat, or the helpless contemplation of others' agony something bearable, supportable'.[12] In war, the responsibility of the chaplain was clear – to sustain a world-view in which the maiming and death of comrades, the results of battle, the imminent threat of a soldier's own demise, and all the incidents of army life, had a recognisable moral purpose. Making sense of imminent suffering and violence in religious terms has always been a challenge, yet religion has repeatedly given hope and strength in the presence of suffering and death.

---

11 See, for example, *A Sermon Preached unto the Voluntiers* [sic] *of the City of Norwich and also to the Volunteers of Great Yarmouth* (London, 1644), 6; Obadiah Sedgwick, *A Thanks-giving Sermon Preached before the Honourable House of Commons at Westminster* (9 April 1644), 23

12 Clifford Geertz, 'Religion as a Cultural System', in *The Interpretation of Cultures: Selected Essays by Clifford Geertz*, New York, NY: Basic Books, 1973, 89ff.

Ireland

It is a legitimate duty of the Christian churches to minister spiritually to those in their care, especially those whose lives are in danger, to console those who are ill and to extend spiritual support to those who are imprisoned. In these respects, generations of chaplains have performed an important role. This was highlighted in the nineteenth century in Ireland when Paul Cullen, as Archbishop of Dublin and Ireland's first cardinal, struggled actively to have Catholic chaplains appointed to a variety of state services, from prisons and the army to various hospitals and branches of social and educational societal care. He repeatedly emphasised how chaplains provided religious support and consolation to those in their charge. His arguments were successful, and by the close of the nineteenth century and the dawn of the twentieth a number of chaplains had been appointed to various sectors of Irish society.

Politics

Historically, chaplains' experiences, insights and influence are noteworthy but should not be overestimated. While the dangers of military chaplains preaching nationalism was repeatedly evident, this same preaching later presented significant challenges for some, especially in the face of defeat in war. Numerous governments attempted to use chaplains as agents of political propaganda. Preaching a message of nationalistic evangelisation had far-reaching consequences as chaplains' prayers implored God for victory, asking for earthly glory and not for salvation. Sometimes they were accused of undermining the Christian belief in forgiveness. In order to fulfil their tasks properly, chaplains over recent generations gradually became aware of the need to keep their distance from politics. In the generations of chaplains since, and including, the time of Cardinal Cullen in the nineteenth century, it has repeatedly been emphasised that the political agenda of national leaders should not be merged with the spiritual task chaplains were called to perform.

From the closing decades of the nineteenth century and the early decades of the twentieth, especially following the founding of the Irish Free State, chaplains gradually came to perform a multiplicity of tasks and assumed numerous secular and administrative responsibilities, both practical as well as spiritual. Some gradually came to be almost all things to all in their charge. While at all times they conducted religious services, celebrated the sacraments, prayed, preached and counselled those in their charge, they also came to assume responsibilities with respect to caring for the sick and the wounded, burying the dead, chronicling the activities of various institutions and functioning as librarians and treasurers on committees, along with numerous teaching, social outreach and academic responsibilities.

World Wars

Earning the respect of those in their charge was often a challenge for some chaplains. General acceptance of the Gospel message, and adherence to the Catholic faith by those in their charge, did not mean that those whom chaplains served, even pious ones, necessarily admired the priest himself. Many soldiers' diaries from the two world wars say little or nothing concerning chaplains that could serve as an indication of how, despite their dedicated service, they were viewed as especially relevant in the eyes of numerous members of the armed forces. Nonetheless, the diaries, and subsequently recorded recollections of chaplains, give an understanding of how chaplains found their roles especially difficult and challenging as they preached, administered the sacraments, soothed the sick and wounded and buried the war dead in the field. These diaries attest to how frequently they were consulted by men struggling with issues of conscience throughout the war.[13]

13 See, for example, John Martin Brennan, *Irish Catholic Chaplains in the First World War*, Birmingham: The University of Birmingham, School of History and Cultures, 2011; Martin Purdy, *Roman Catholic Army Chaplains During the First World War: Roles, Experiences and Dilemmas,* Preston, Lancs: University of Central Lancashire, 2012; Duff Crerar, 'In the Day of Battle: Canadian Catholic Chaplains in the Field, 1885–1945', CCHA, *Historical Studies*, 61 (1995), 53–77; John Bickersteth (ed.), *The Bickersteth Diaries, 1914–1918,* London: Leo Cooper, 1995.

Military chaplains served on both sides over the course of both world wars in the twentieth century. Experience has proven how early in war, with the prospect of victory imminent, the services arranged by the military chaplains were often well attended. Interestingly, history records the relationship between the increasing duration of war and the increasingly challenging tasks encountered by the military chaplains. Chaplains and soldiers alike were confronted with the horrors of modern warfare, with hundreds of soldiers killed and injured, month after month, while many of those who survived were either severely mutilated or traumatised. Both soldiers and chaplains had to find ways of coping with the challenges of the situation. As their predecessors had done in the past, numerous chaplains in both world wars delivered sermons encouraging soldiers to continue fighting to the bitter end. Following both defeats, military chaplains in Germany faced widespread hostility as the political vision that they represented lost credibility. Soldiers, filled with endless grief and coping with such horrors presented almost insurmountable challenges to chaplains reaching out to those in their care.

The Trenches

Although many wrote of how they found war service harrowing, chaplains' letters, reports and diaries show little disillusionment or loss of faith. Many of those who expressed their views about the war, the Gospel and the mission of the Church echoed the military idealism of pre-war days. Some chaplains came to appreciate, admire and even idealise the trench ethic of comradeship. It was rarely the war, but more often the subsequent return of peacetime that disillusioned the chaplains. Men returning from the front of the First World War found Ireland, in particular, a very different country from the one they left, due to the 1916 Rising and its aftermath.

Theology

Following the wars of the twentieth century, numerous chaplains have reflected on the necessary distance between the world of politics and war on the one side, and the world of spiritual care and consolation on the other. Some chaplains who witnessed and experienced the finer aspects of courage and sacrifice that emerged during the war later aimed to remember the heroism and the deeper lessons that shone through. The public image of the non-combatant chaplain, during the decade after the wars, was a positive one overall. Usually, the chaplain was portrayed as the medical officer's alter ego, a spiritual officer who was brave, devoted, patriotic and useful for passing out cigarettes and helping with letters. Once united by war, some chaplains, however, found themselves on opposite sides of post-war disputes. Paul Tillich, the influential Protestant theologian and a military chaplain in the First World War, wrote of how he struggled to define the precise service he was meant to deliver. Was fighting for one's fatherland the way to gain eternal salvation? True love, he maintained, was reflected in one's readiness to sacrifice one's life for those one loved. Tillich's theology grew and developed with time and, as the war progressed, he moved from preaching ultimate loyalty to one's king to ultimate loyalty to Christ.[14]

Contemporary Ireland

In Ireland, from the time of Cardinal Cullen in the mid-nineteenth century through to recent decades, the range and breadth of chaplaincies developed significantly. To military and prison chaplaincy were added dedicated chaplaincy services to both second- and third-level institutions. Chaplaincy services for hospitals, prisons, ports and airports, international communities, seafarers, emigrants, migrants and members of the Traveller community, among many others, were developed. National chaplaincies evolved for sectors of Irish society ranging from a chaplaincy to members of the Garda Síochána to chaplaincies to those who are deaf or have particular needs.

In contemporary Ireland, chaplains continue to serve the community,

---

14 Cf. Lon Weaver, *Religious Internationalism: War and Peace in the Thought of Paul Tillich*, Macon, GA: Mercer University Press, 1984.

frequently as members of pastoral care teams who are especially conscious that to be fully human, all are called to function and grow cognitively, physiologically, psychologically, emotionally, societally and spiritually in an integrated manner. Their role is often a challenging, supportive and sensitive one as they animate and assist people to articulate their spirituality and strive to respond to the spiritual lives of those in their care. Chaplaincy, now increasingly situated within the context of pastoral care teams, offers a full range of spiritual services, frequently responding to the profound spiritual and emotional needs of those in their care. This is achieved through their ability to listen and support those dealing with powerlessness, pain and alienation. Chaplaincies and pastoral teams today aim to provide a holistic approach by empowering others to draw upon the strengths of spirituality to meet the challenges of their lives. Their calling recognises how each person is precious and how Christ calls every person to fullness of life.

Chaplains can act as catalysts in assisting those to whom they minister; facilitating self-reflection and the ability to draw on inner strengths and coping mechanisms in the face of life, to change what can be changed and to cope positively and peacefully with that which cannot. They do so through various pathways from listening and prayer, celebrating sacraments, leading series of retreats and liturgies, to offering public prayer, to name but a few. Many are specifically trained to provide spiritual and practical counselling by means of accredited clinical pastoral educational courses. Committed to the values of Christ, the chaplain, on behalf of the Church, accompanies each person on the journey through life. Chaplains' listening presence and support in pastoral offices are appreciated by contemporary society.

Faith-filled

Chaplaincy is a faith-filled path and the pastoral teams with which chaplains journey are drawn from a wide-ranging skill-base, religious and lay, ordained and non-ordained, many of whom hold qualifications in theology, religious studies, pastoral studies or spirituality from accredited institutions. Animated by a close relationship to Christ, every chaplain is charged with respecting and accepting others. Given the demands of the posting, it is important that they are adequately supported, rooting themselves in, and availing of, opportunities for personal prayer as well as spiritual and religious awareness and development. A dedicated spiritual director, supervisor or counsellor for chaplains is increasingly recognised as important. Chaplains are required to have solid theological foundations, which are critical in the context of their requirements to adhere to all safeguarding norms without compromise while exercising respect for all faith views.

Looking to the Future

Today, there are increasing calls for chaplaincies to accommodate the growing numbers of small faith groups that desire to be registered to respond to the increasing religious diversity in society. In recent decades, census figures in Ireland indicate that growing numbers of people strive to live a more secular, personal, humanistic spirituality whilst exploring the ultimate values of love, meaning, hope, beauty and truth.

The role of the chaplain from the days of the Roman Empire to contemporary times has evolved and grown. At its heart lies a commitment to the person of Jesus Christ and the message of the Gospel. Among the aims of chaplains down the centuries has been the creation of a culture of spiritual encounter and care, accompaniment and hope, reflection and action. Being present and listening, while caring for the community, are still a major part of the lives of chaplains. As their role in society is evaluated anew it is hoped that those who are chaplains in the Ireland of the future will build on the positives of the past, learn from the mistakes of previous generations and help to better promote the building of the Kingdom of God on earth that all pray for when they recite the 'Our Father'.

5: The Encounter at the Well: A Model for Chaplaincy

Eileen O'Connell

'Encounter is a first step toward solidarity. This involves a dynamic and complex process that moves from encounter to accompaniment over time. Showing up for others over time builds trust, creating the conditions for people to authentically share in meaningful exchange.'
Marcus Mescher[1]

'The enterprise is exploration into God'[2]

How does one offer a scriptural reflection on chaplaincy when the Scriptures contain no instances of chaplaincy? It goes without saying that there are no chaplains in the entirety of the Bible! Nevertheless, the ministry of chaplaincy is rooted in biblical tradition, and reflection on it must be through the lens of Scripture. Numerous passages, too many to mention, shed light on various elements of chaplaincy and reflect the values that underpin the ministry. I have chosen to focus on a peculiar encounter at a well between a thirsty Jesus and a woman from Samaria, recounted in John's Gospel (4:4–42). Its key details are familiar to most but there is more that is less well known.

Why have I chosen this episode in Jesus' ministry? This encounter unfolds in three phases: (1) Two strangers meet and each shows hospitality; (2) through conversation, new insight and understanding are reached; (3) with new vistas opened, new disciples are made and existing disciples are challenged. These overlap somewhat so that the boundaries between them are blurred. A similar dynamic is evident in the

---

1   Marcus Mescher, *The Ethics of Encounter: Christian Neighbor Love as a Practice of Solidarity*, Maryknoll, NY: Orbis Books, 2020 (Kindle edition), 105.
2   Christopher Fry, *A Sleep of Prisoners*, 1951.

ministry of chaplaincy. The three phases encapsulate three aspects that I consider central to chaplaincy: attentive presence, opening new vistas and missionary discipleship. While this passage can serve as a template for many aspects of the Christian journey, here it is applied to an exploration of chaplaincy.

The Samaritan Woman

What happens in this text? John presents a very human Jesus. He is out of place – in Samaritan land, not Jewish territory. At the hottest part of the day and 'tired out by his journey', he sits at Jacob's well. He is dependent on others for his needs – namely, his disciples to bring food and a stranger to quench his thirst. All he can do is wait, because 'the well is deep' and he has no bucket. When the Samaritan woman arrives, Jesus' first words to her are to request her help. Jesus is not the one in control here, initially at least, and perhaps he expects nothing more than to be given the water he needs. The unusual dynamic of this encounter is evident from the outset. While the woman is surprised that a Jewish man speaks to her, that he does so is not what is most remarkable. Far more interesting is the nature of the conversation and its outcome. Theirs is a robust exchange that is both awkward and significant. It is awkward because they spar verbally, particularly at the start, but this is what allows their conversation to become significant, to deepen and go beyond the immediate, to shift from Jesus' very human need for water to her human need for more than daily existence. Despite its shaky beginning, by its end a disciple has emerged and she calls others to discipleship.

'Give me a drink'

'Give me a drink' (John 4:7). This is where the conversation begins and it does not start promisingly. Perhaps caught off guard, the Samaritan's first words are far from gracious: 'How is it that you, a Jew, ask … me, a woman of Samaria?' She seems baffled, but Jesus models a wide understanding of hospitality and attentive presence. Undeterred, he

61

continues, answering with a retort of his own and asserts that he has 'living water'. Taking literally what Jesus says about water, her words appear to contain a sarcastic put-down: 'You have no bucket.' But there is genuine questioning here too and she is curious, seeking to know more. It is to her curiosity that Jesus responds, twice telling of other water, 'that I will give'. Again, taking him literally, she asks for some, because it would quench her thirst and end her tiresome daily chore of 'coming here to draw water'.

Taking place in the noonday heat, their lengthy exchange is, in one sense, a waste of time. Some might say this is a very poor example of time management in terms of securing a simple drink of water! Jesus seems in a conversational, if not argumentative, mood. He might have responded to her surprise in a less combative manner, received water and, his thirst eased, waited for the disciples. Initially, the Samaritan seems unwelcoming, yet, we must assume, does not refuse to provide the simple hospitality of a drink to Jesus. She could then have shared water, refilled her bucket and returned to the cool of her home. Yet this is not what happens. Both invest time in this encounter so that it becomes far more than a simple request for water. Despite their differences, neither shirks discussion, even in the heat! Instead, fully present to one another and willing to speak and listen, to ask and answer questions, they move beyond what separates them to engage with one another. This is an instance of hospitality even though there is neither host nor guest and the provision of refreshments is no more than a minor feature. Far more significant are other elements of hospitality that are evident here: spending time in the company of another, the sharing of insights and the unfolding of ideas and beliefs in conversation, i.e. attentive presence.

This is what creates space for and leads to a deeper level of discussion, one that enables people to reach mutual understanding. Shortly, Jesus and the woman will move from the relatively safe and neutral topic of water to the far more personal question of her life. From being a potentially inconsequential interaction, it deepens and becomes quite significant. It shows all too clearly that any meeting can lead to more than is anticipated. This is true for chaplaincy too. It begins in small talk but does not end there.

Attentive Presence

Attentive presence, made concrete in hospitality and welcome, is both a key part of Christian mission and an expression of it. It is also intrinsic to the nature of the triune God. Where we see this, God is at work. In all of its forms, chaplaincy must articulate this welcome and hospitality, this characteristic of God so often revealed in the Scriptures. It must do this in a manner that is inclusive and welcoming of all people, regardless of their belief or lack thereof. It cannot exclude.

Hospitality and welcome is not a means to an end but a way of being. It is expressed in many ways. This is foundational: that those at home in God are welcoming of others and invite them to find their home or to consider further where their home might be.

In chaplaincy, hospitality and welcome, attentive presence and availability form the bedrock that enables – and nurtures – encounter, engagement and connection. This is hard work and it demands time and effort and plenty of both. Yet it is something that happens not by doing but by being. Involving a stance of radical availability rather than activism, it is about showing up, being open to and holding a space for what might happen. It asks for a degree of flexibility and detachment from ideas about productivity and pre-set agendas. This requires not a full diary but the willingness to invest in waiting and in wasting time. It demands that chaplains not appear overly occupied, too busy to approach, but the opposite – that we[3] make a commitment to 'loiter with intent' – to borrow the phrase of my Dominican confrère Brother Timothy Radcliffe. We must be prepared to recognise that, as chaplains, we are both hosts and guests, gifted with the hospitality of those who generously and courageously share their lives and their stories with us, and learning from

3   For the sake of clarity, throughout this chapter the word 'we' is used to refer to chaplains and 'they' when referring to those to whom chaplains minister.

them and from what they open our eyes to in their sharing. It necessitates an acknowledgement of interdependency and an acceptance that we do not have all the resources, all the answers, but need what others can offer us too, knowing that we can be nourished by this. It calls us to patience, to realising that, even if we imagine that we know what comes next, we cannot force outcomes. Rather we must wait, allowing God to work in God's own time (Mark 4:27).

From this starting place of hospitality and welcome, of inviting others to relationship, we show something of our God who 'so loved the world' (John 3:16). We reflect too on the breaking down of barriers between people of which Paul wrote (Galatians 3:28; Colossians 3:11; Ephesians 2:13–17). We cannot be lavish enough in our hospitality but are to be generous, even wasteful, with our welcome, indiscriminately showing goodness and kindness with no expectations attached, loving and serving without seeking reciprocation. An attitude that is both loving and non-judgemental is paramount.

From a Christian perspective, being this way reflects the loving communion of the Trinity. The positive possibilities of our being thus are numerous. We can show what it is to be people who know God's love and we are called to communicate this to others. This is a language that may not speak to them. We preach best when our lives witness that God's invitation is to everyone. Being chaplains in this manner can create community open to welcoming and including everyone. Only when we invest our time, make ourselves available, work to build trust, can those we minister to and walk alongside be authentically themselves. They can be genuine in what they share with us, open and honest, and free to ask their real questions. We can truly encounter the other person and they can encounter us. Experiencing attentive presence, being seen, heard and accepted as they are, can allow people to see things differently, to perceive the opening of a new vista. Relationships of trust bring the opportunity for deeper conversations to develop in an unforced manner, moving from the mundane and trivial to what is real and important and perhaps venturing into previously unexplored and unimagined topics.

This is what happens to the Samaritan woman. It happens when people meet with Jesus. It can happen today too. When it does, it is almost always transformative in some way.

'Go, call your husband'

Up to this point, Jesus and the Samaritan woman have engaged in riddle-like talk about water and thirst. She is somewhat confused by what he says but this small talk, superficial as it seems, is an essential starting point. Suddenly, the conversation between them takes an unexpected turn. Now Jesus makes it personal, really piquing her interest. When he changes the subject, the conversation begins to become real. Now, it is about her and about her life. Now, what is said does matter. He instructs her to call her husband (John 4:16). Undaunted, she offers an honest answer: 'I have no husband.' Hearing Jesus describe her life and speak of her five husbands[4] pushes her further in her efforts to understand what he is revealing to her.[5] This is not an interaction that bludgeons her into a change of perspective but rather an open and respectful dialogue. As they talk, the woman of Samaria moves towards a new understanding. She realises there is more to this man than she thought: 'I see that you are a prophet.' Their conversation moves to another, more profound level. She poses theological questions about aspects of their respective beliefs, sharing with Jesus what she believes and has been taught and seeking to understand his Jewish perspective. Jesus' answer leads her to share her Samaritan expectations of the Messiah. Jesus affirms her description and declares openly: 'I am he' (John 4:26). She makes no reply.

Without saying it to him, she makes a connection between the Messiah

4   This is a literal reading of the text. For exegetical discussion of the different motifs, see for example, Sandra M. Schneiders, *Written That You May Believe: Encountering Jesus in the Fourth Gospel* (rev. ed.), New York, NY: Herder & Herder, 2003; Francis J. Moloney, *The Gospel of John,* Sacra Pagina, Daniel J. Harrington SJ (ed.), no. 4 (rev. ed.), Collegeville, MN: The Liturgical Press, 2005.

5   Schneiders, op. cit., describes the Samaritan woman as, 'a genuine theological dialogue partner gradually experiencing Jesus' self-revelation even as she reveals herself to him'(at 41).

and this Jewish stranger. It is an outcome that is entirely unanticipated. Yet this extraordinary episode takes place in a very ordinary human reality. A man, tired and thirsty, sits waiting for his friends. This mundaneness is where the wellside conversation begins, one that changes the lives of the woman and many Samaritans of Sychar. This stop on their journey also opens up the disciples to new insights.

Opening New Vistas

Likewise with chaplaincy, this potential to move from surface-level chat to deeper layers of conversation exists. While today's well could be a coffee shop or the myriad other locations where people come together and encounter one another, chaplaincy is somehow qualitatively different. Chaplaincy is both like many other places and, at the same time, more. The added ingredient, one that sets it apart and is at its core, is the faith perspective of the chaplain. The chaplain's faith is in God and as such their work is God's work.

It is in this quite ordinary place, albeit a space that makes room for and welcomes out-of-the-ordinary encounter, that people can begin to perceive the extraordinary and gain greater clarity regarding what is significant to them. In my short experience of university chaplaincy, it was the time spent over cups of tea with the chaplain that opened opportunities for students to seek out a deeper conversation about things that matter in life. It is a well in more than one sense, offering nourishment on many levels. It can open a space to detect something previously imperceptible, prompt a shift in perspective, offer language and opportunity to discern an alternative view of reality.

Many today are uncomfortable with the existence of people who do not share their opinions but hold opposing positions. They experience not only their points of view but the people themselves as threatening. Either they struggle to engage or avoid it altogether, remaining in communication only with those with whom they agree. Chaplains need to ensure that chaplaincy does not fall prey to this danger, turning in on itself and being closed off from other points of view. A time of echo chambers and polarising discourse needs people who show an authentic desire to befriend those that think differently about life and who seek to understand their alternative perspectives, even if not necessarily agreeing with or adopting their stance. It calls for an openness to seeing other possibilities and an ability to hold tensions in order to make possible a space where what unites can be discerned. Pope Francis writes that the Spirit 'always preserves the legitimate plurality of different groups and points of view, reconciling them in their diversity'.[6]

This is not a simple task, nor one with an immediate outcome. To do this necessitates attentive presence along with places for encounters that are enriching rather than threatening. It requires both the time and desire to put in the necessary effort. In a world that is always busy and rushed, people with time on their hands who are willing to spend it with others are a source of curiosity. It is this availability that makes them attractive.

Chaplains can be such people – 'holy loiterers'! When we are thus, we are a reminder that to engage in difficult conversations is not only possible but necessary. Today, it is imperative that we do not retreat into silos where people think as we do, but rather that we go beyond these comfortable spaces in order to engage with those with whom we disagree, with those with whom we do not wish to speak or who do not wish to speak with us. It requires trust in God's plan for a future built on unity rather than division and on acceptance of diversity as richness and not something divisive. Speaking to the woman of Samaria, Jesus describes what the realisation of this plan will look like: 'true worshippers will worship the Father in spirit and in truth.' They are no longer separated by an attachment to place that is divisive. In what happens between Jesus and this woman and in what follows, there are hints that this hoped-for future is already breaking through.

The truths Jesus reveals about her life and his identity represent an invitation that requires a decision on her part, either to dismiss him or

6   Pope Francis, *Let Us Dream: The Path to a Better Future*, London: Simon & Schuster, 2020, 65.

to be changed. Choosing the latter, she first makes a leap outside her existing belief. A Samaritan woman recognises a Jewish man as the Messiah. Next, she becomes a disciple.

Today, too, in encounters that offer a new vista, there is an invitation. Whether one decides to accept or decline, one must choose. To accept means that action follows. Then, those encounters are transformative. They propel us beyond ourselves and our concerns. They create disciples, people willing to share with others their sense of life as gift, to offer a glimpse of the 'more' that they have experienced and that has enriched them. This is not limited to those who, like the woman from Samaria, meet Jesus in person. Today, too, it is possible for chaplains to offer the possibility of an encounter with Jesus.

'Come and see'

The Samaritan woman returns to Sychar, not with her water jar, but as a disciple and as a missionary in her own place, preaching Jesus to the people. Her meeting with Jesus has radically altered her perspective. In response, she becomes a disciple, eager to share this new understanding with her own Samaritan people (John 4:29). She goes without fear to tell them that, in this Jew, she has found the Messiah, the one that they in their faith have anticipated. Such is her enthusiasm and conviction that they, in turn, come to believe and return with her to Jesus, declaring him 'the Saviour of the world'.

Meanwhile, the twelve get it wrong. In their thinking, the disciples have placed borders around Jesus and defined limits as to whom he can speak with or where he can minister. Jesus operates from a broader understanding of discipleship than they do. When they return, their reaction is telling. They are 'astonished' and disapprove wordlessly of Jesus' company. Perhaps they are even more 'astonished' when he speaks of a harvest among people who are not Jews. Indicating that his work extends beyond them and beyond Judea, Jesus reorients the disciples' perspective and broadens their narrow understanding of him. Elsewhere, too, the disciples seek to make distinctions between people. Each time, Jesus corrects their misapprehension and gently widens their horizons. Jesus welcomes everyone to conversation. Some become disciples, others reject him. Response notwithstanding, he is not deterred from speaking with and inviting others to relationship. Following him is open to all and no one is to be turned away (Matthew 19:13–14; Luke 9:49–50; Mark 9:38–39; later Paul addresses this; see Galatians 3:28). The possibility of an encounter that awakens people to a deeper understanding or new perspectives is offered to everyone. Neither disciples then nor disciples now are gatekeepers to God or Jesus. As Pope Francis puts it, 'the Church is not a border station', and we cannot 'put up "do not enter" signs'.[7]

Missionary Discipleship

Chaplains are disciples already. At the heart of our identity is that we are people of faith. Our relationship with God is the ground on which we stand, the place from which we can be an attentive presence offering to others hospitality and welcome. When chaplains are available to others in this way, deep encounters can occur and possibilities for new ways of seeing and of living are opened up. But this does not depend on the giftedness or charisma of the chaplain. What is important in the ministry of chaplaincy is that we are with people where they are, accompanying, encouraging and supporting them. Of itself, engagement – forming relationships with people and identifying with them as best we can – is a form of preaching, one that recognises Christ in the other. Chaplains are merely conduits of God's grace. It is God already present who does the work.

To become disciples, we need to meet Jesus, to know him and to realise that we are known and loved by him. This changes us. We cannot keep the impact of discovering Jesus to ourselves. Compelled to invite others to share in this, we carry Jesus with us, bringing the Good News

7   Pope Francis, 'Homily of His Holiness Pope Francis, Enrique Olaya Herrera airport, Saturday, 9 September 2017', https://www.vatican.va/content/francesco/en/ homilies/2017/ documents/papa-francesco_20170909_omelia-viaggioapostolico-colombiamed ellin.html.

to others and seeking to bring others to him. This occurred in Samaria. Leaving behind her water jar, the woman carries her experience of Jesus to the Samaritan town, going to tell others about Jesus and bringing them to him so that they share in this.

To remain a disciple, ongoing relationship with Jesus is essential. The Samaritan woman returns to spend more time with Jesus. Those townspeople with her invite Jesus to stay with them. Today, our relationship with Jesus is built in and on prayer. In this aspect of discipleship, Jesus is our teacher. The gospels recount numerous instances of Jesus praying to his Father. Perseverance in prayer is what empowers us and sustains us as disciples. The demands of discipleship are many and not insignificant.

If chaplaincy is a place and space with potential to draw people towards discipleship, forming and equipping disciples is an important aspect. Imparting skills is not of greatest significance here. Rather, it is how we are that matters and that attracts others. It is important to remember the maxim that faith is caught, not taught. Something similar holds for discipleship. Chaplains whose lives show integrity and coherence are far more effective at modelling discipleship than any efforts to proselytise. Indeed, the latter is most likely counter-productive and off-putting. When the centrality of prayer in our lives is evident, when it is clear that we do not just speak *about* but *to* God, we can have something to say to others. When others see us make time for prayer, they can see our desire for relationship with Jesus and our ongoing commitment to seeking to know him more and to be changed by him (Romans 12:2). It points to that which underpins our *raison d'être* as persons and that of our ministry as chaplains. More fundamentally, it teaches that just as we need prayer in order to be sustained in our ministry, they need this too. If we are not in touch with God, we can be only lukewarm disciples.

It is this, perhaps, that is of greatest importance in helping to form missionary disciples who are ablaze with the love of Jesus, whom they have met, and ready to share this with others. This is what best equips them to witness to those they meet and to offer them the hospitality and attentive presence that they have received through the ministry of chaplains. Yet, on its own, seeing us model this is not sufficient. We also witness to other aspects of discipleship that enable discipleship in others.

The onus is on us, as chaplains, to maintain connection with people, not only in the hope that disciples emerge but to ensure that they can grow. Our willingness and availability to reach and engage with people allows us see their gifts, to help them to recognise these and to encourage them as they put them to use in the world around them.

In the context where chaplaincy is with students, for example, there is a fine balance to be struck between being responsive to and being led by them, on the one hand, and on the other, being willing to prod students and guide them to go further. It is an opportunity for building social responsibility. As much as it is about presence and accompaniment and opening up spaces for bigger conversations, it is also about encouraging them to reach beyond their comfort zones, to seek out conversations with others, and to be disciples wherever they find themselves.[8]

Conclusion

Jesus models presence, availability and hospitality throughout his public life. The encounter in Samaria is just one instance. It is no accident that so much of what is recorded of the life of Jesus centres on food, meals, hospitality. He is disparaged as 'a glutton and a drunkard' and 'a friend of tax collectors and sinners' (Matthew 11:19), always eating and not always with the 'right people'. The 'bread of life' meets people around the table, eating with those who like him and with those who are marginalised or have marginalised themselves. He shows us an alternative vision. From among those who accept him, he commissions disciples to go and do likewise. As followers of Christ, people who have met him, have made a home in him, have seen the alternative life on offer and, in that, discovered a vocation to live as his disciples, chaplains must imitate Christ.

---

8   Clearly, this is not restricted solely to chaplaincy with students but also applies in many
     other contexts where chaplains minister.

Chaplains have been blessed and our place is a privileged one. It is holy ground. Like Abraham, we are blessed by God to be a blessing, persons of faith tasked with working 'alongside' God (Genesis 12:2–3). Our task is not to determine who belongs among those we are to accompany. We have no need to worry about that. We welcome God in and through all those whom we encounter (Genesis 18:1–15; Matthew 25:3–6, 40; Hebrews 13:2). If the Kingdom of Heaven is a lavish banquet where all are welcome (Isaiah 25:6; Matthew 22:1–14), then generous hospitality that fosters and builds relationship and invites everyone is key. We are to bless indiscriminately and lavishly without pausing to ask whether the people we meet share our beliefs and our perspective or are likely to reject both these and us. This is what Jesus does and we must do likewise.

6: The Chaplain:
An Essential Element of Education

Ronan Barry

*'In the course of their journey young people look for someone who ...
will know how to speak to their hearts ... will know how to speak to
them about the problems which worry them, and propose solutions,
values perspectives which are worth staking one's future on.'*
Saint Pope John Paul II, World Day for Vocations, 1995

Introduction

For many educational communities, faith has been fundamental
to their foundation and their ongoing mission. Given the current
environment,[1] where many people question the value and relevance
of faith-based education, it is clear that Catholic education and
other denominational educational programmes have kept the Gospel
values central to their mission. It is faithfulness to these values lived
out in specific ways at particular times that gives our educational
communities their special charism. Faith-based education today continues
to endeavour to develop its unique identity or 'characteristic spirit' in the
context of current times.

Supporting Personal and Faith Development in the Current Context

*Before the Covid experience, I would probably travel through an airport
at least once a year. Every time I went to the airport, I travelled through
security, customs and passport control like clockwork. Then I travelled
on to the luggage belt to collect my bag. It is a brilliant system. I, along*

---

1   Shauna Bowers, 'Religion should be taught outside school hours, campaigners say', *Irish
    Times*, https://www.irishtimes.com/news/education/religion-should-be-taught-outside-
    school-hours-campaigners-say-1.4030376.

with many other people, am happy with this system. No matter what country you were in it was the same. Language was not a barrier, it was seamless. Then one day you arrive at the luggage belt and you wait, and nothing comes out.

I came across this analogous story (parable) during a conversation with a colleague regarding the transmission of faith. As communities of faith, we have had systems for many generations that have sustained the transmission of faith. The faith development of every person originates in the family experience but is supported by the parish community and the school community. Faith has been handed on from generation to generation through these systems for centuries. However, in many areas of our world today, the system no longer works. In a sense, we are left waiting for our luggage.

Numerous young people today no longer accept the beliefs of their parents and/or their Church.[2] Many want to travel life's journey in a way that is authentic and supports their search for meaning. Young people who are searching for meaning seem to want to understand God's plan in a personal manner and not just through the lens of an educational institution, and/or the Church.[3]

This supports the observation that society is growing secular in nature and is pushing religion and belief into the private sphere. Brian Flannery, the former Irish Jesuit Education executive officer, observes, 'As Christianity slowly disappears from the wider culture, there is a comparable erosion of Catholic identity within the School',[4] and he continues,

> In this new scenario rather than promote a particular identity, the school downplays all identity in an effort to be neutral and inclusive. Religious viewpoints become a private matter and

2   Gareth Byrne and Leslie J. Francis (eds), *Religion and Education: The Voices of Young People in Ireland,* Dublin: Veritas Publications, 2019, 280.
3   Ibid., 133.
4   Brian Flannery, *Studies,* Vol. 108, no. 429, 48.

the school avoids all discourse around its founding mission …

Religion instruction is abandoned.[5]

Instead of shying away from this culture of secularism, Pope Francis puts the encounter with Jesus at the centre of everything Christian. This encounter leads to a new space where Pope Francis dreams of a missionary option.[6] Francis puts discipleship and mission as the two pillars of transforming and uniting the Church into the future.[7] In *Evangelii Gaudium* he calls for the initiation of a process where a new space can evolve and develop to the point of 'bearing fruit'.[8]

In a post-resurrection world, Jesus' followers transformed the society they lived in by participating in the *Missio Dei* (God's Mission). Like them, we are living in a world in transition, as articulated by Pope Francis: 'We are no longer in an era of change but a change of era'.[9] In this context the role of the chaplain in education is essential. The chaplain becomes the link, the bridge builder, between a member of an educational community and the community of faith. The school chaplain becomes a lived connection between young people searching for meaning but living in the milieu of change. The chaplain's contribution to young people can bring the wisdom and insight of a faith tradition to the context of their world today.

Archbishop Michael Jackson, in an online presentation to chaplaincy students, declares, 'Chaplaincy enables authorised people of faith to go where an institutional Church can perhaps not go at all and can perhaps not go as quickly.'[10] For Luke Monahan and Caroline Renehan, the school chaplain is an authorised presence who, rooted in a particular situation as 'a faith presence, committed to the values of Christ, and on behalf of

5   Ibid.
6   *Evangelli Gaudium*, 27.
7   Ibid., 20–45.
8   Ibid., 223.
9   Papal address to representatives of the Fifth National Conference of the Italian Church, 2015.
10   'Chaplaincy Students Have Virtual Visit from Archbishop', United Dioceses of Dublin & Glendalough, https://dublin.anglican.org/news/2020/04/29/chaplaincy-students-have-virtual-visit.

the church and school, accompanies each person on the journey through life'.[11] They also observe that 'Chaplains in schools are key players in the delivery of the education.'[12]

Beyond the expected contributors to the understanding of chaplaincy it is worth noting that the Supreme Court's conclusion, through Justice Barrington, to a hearing with regard to the state's provision of chaplains in community schools declared, 'The role of the chaplain is to help to provide this extra dimension to the religious education of the children.'[13]

Monaghan and Renehan's statements and the Supreme Court's ruling are significant as they indicate that the role of a chaplain is a key element in the delivery of a denominational education. Both statements go to the heart of chaplaincy as a faith presence that is a lived experience rooted in relationships and expressed in the delivery of a holistic educational programme for all.

The annual publication of school league tables[14] in national and local media saddens many educationalists. The general acceptance of these league tables as indicators of a successful education is misplaced. Academic results are not an indicator in themselves of a welcoming, caring and nurturing environment where students reach their personal and academic potential. Educational engagement, through teaching and learning, clearly goes to the core of the school's mission, but students' achievements cannot and should not be indicated by academic results alone.

There are many social, environmental and cultural factors that influence these results. In 2019 Focus Ireland and the Irish National Teachers' Organisation (INTO) highlighted the challenges of homelessness in education. We know from national and international research the impact

---

11 Luke Monahan and Caroline Renehan, *The Chaplain: A Faith Presence In The School Community*, Dublin: Columba Press, 1998, 13.
12 Ibid.
13 Supreme Court Campaign to separate Church and State, 1998, 2 *ILRM*, 101.
14 Katherine Donnelly, 'Feeder Schools League Tables 2020: How your local school fared', *Irish Independent*, https://www.independent.ie/irish-news/education/feeder-schools-league-tables-2020-how-your-local-school-fared-39944810.html (accessed 16 May 2021).

of homelessness on children's education. In particular, the stress and practical difficulties of living in emergency or temporary accommodation mean that children are not arriving at school ready to learn.[15]

For most parents preparing to send their children to a school, the institutional culture and core values have a weighted importance that goes beyond league table results.[16] It must always be remembered that faith education is not determined as a success or failure purely on its results. Faith-based educational communities are places of learning and locations where values are communicated and shared.

Second-level Education Provision Overview

Included in the Education Act (1998), which governs the management of schools in Ireland, we find the following statement:

> I ... school shall provide education to students which is appropriate to their abilities and needs and, without prejudice to the generality of the foregoing, it shall use its available resources to – ensure that the educational needs of all students, including those with a disability or other special educational needs, are identified and provided for ... (d) promote the moral, spiritual, social and personal development of students and provide health education for them, in consultation with their parents, having regard to the characteristic spirit of the school.[17]

In Ireland, to deliver these aspects of education and all others, three main models of secondary education provision are employed.

1. Community colleges are established by the local Education and Training Board (ETB), which is also the sole patron of the school. Community colleges are funded by the Department of Education and Science through the ETBs and deliver the post-primary

---

15 'Homelessness in the Classroom: A resource for primary schools', Focus Ireland, www.focusireland.ie/wp-content/uploads/2019/08/Homelessness-in-the-Classroom.pdf.
16 Maura Hyland (ed.), *Why Send Your Child to a Catholic School?* Dublin: Veritas Publications, 2013, 81.
17 Education Act 1998, Section 9, www.irishstatutebook.ie/eli/1998/act/51/section/9/enacted/en/html (accessed 17 May 2021).

curriculum.

2. Community schools are established, either by one or more private or religious patrons coming together with an ETB patron, or as the result of the amalgamation of voluntary secondary and ETB schools. Community Schools are also funded by the Department of Education and Science to deliver the post-primary curriculum.

3. Finally, there are voluntary secondary schools, which are privately owned and managed post-primary schools, usually under the patronage of an individual body such as a religious community, a charitable educational trust or a private charitable company. Voluntary secondary schools are funded by the Department of Education and Science to deliver the curriculum. However, it is also important to note some voluntary secondary schools are also fee-charging.

Between 1970 and 2015, the total number of second-level schools declined from 905 to 732, while total enrolment increased from 209,812 to 372,295. In the same period the number of voluntary secondary schools fell from 599 to 375, with enrolment increasing from 150,642 to 191,144. Of the 375 voluntary secondary schools fifty-three are fee-charging (twenty of which are non-Catholic).

This trend indicates that voluntary secondary schools (faith schools) are declining in Ireland. Apart from the odd exception, most schools built or being developed today are state-run. In time, parents who are seeking a faith-based secondary education for their children will find it more difficult to find a school that can meet their needs.

The Vatican Congregation for Catholic Education's 2009 statement on their vision of education offers directions and insight for all involved in Catholic education and other denominational educational programmes. The statement itself offers parameters to Catholic schools, but also for the engagement of Catholic educational bodies with partners (governmental or otherwise) in the provision of education for young people today.

Education is a complex task, which is made more difficult

by rapid social, economic, and cultural changes. Its specific mission remains the integral formation of the human person. Children and young people must be guaranteed the possibility of developing harmoniously their own physical, moral, intellectual, and spiritual gifts, and they must also be helped to develop their sense of responsibility, learn the correct use of freedom, and participate actively in social life.[18]

Chaplaincy in Transition

Alongside the transition in education, there has been a parallel transition in school chaplaincy. In 1976 the School Chaplain's Association was founded under the guidance of Fr Sean Ó Lóinigh, a Limerick diocesan priest, with their first meeting in that same year. At that time, most of the members were ordained clergy and members of religious orders.

In contemporary Ireland, schools have transferred their chaplaincy and pastoral ministry teams to lay people. These chaplains are supported by the educational mission of a particular congregation and/ or an Educational Trust as well as by their own skills, competencies, commitment and enthusiasm. Enthusiasm originates in the the Greek word *enthousiasmos,* meaning 'divine inspiration'. As an example of this transition, the majority of the 156 full-time chaplaincy posts allocated by the Department of Education and Science to ETB secondary schools are filled by qualified lay people.

The chaplain, educationalist and author, John Caperon, observed that 'The sheer diversity is reflected online, and this indicates the dynamic, shifting nature of this ministry today. Since the beginning of the twenty-first century, there has been a rapid and largely uncharted growth in all varieties of Chaplaincy'.[19]

A Chaplain as Presence

18 Congregation for Catholic Education, *Circular Letter to the Presidents of Bishops' Con-ferences on Religious Education in Schools*, www.vatican.va/roman_curia/congregations/ ccatheduc/documents/rc_con_ccatheduc_doc_20090505_circ-insegn-relig_en.html.
19 John Caperon, *A Vital Ministry – Chaplaincy in Schools in the Post-Christian Era*, London: SCM Press, 2015, 1.

Central to a faith-based educational mission is the care of the young person's well-being. Well-being in this case is their social, emotional, physical, spiritual and academic welfare. Chaplains work in this context and their presence in this environment is significant. What do we mean by a chaplain's presence to young people in an education setting?

A working definition of a chaplain's presence includes 'a process through which the chaplain creates an atmosphere of ease and trust so that the recipients of the chaplain's care can share their own story in an environment that is non-judgemental and compassionate.'[20] However, first the chaplain must be fully aware of their own story. Thomas Grenham suggests that 'Effective pastoral presence is characterised by a capacity to translate our own theology and spirituality'[21] to support and accompany people on life's pilgrimage. Not alone should chaplains be present to the context they serve, they must personally witness to their own faith and belief. Through this personal commitment chaplains root themselves in the ministry of Jesus Christ as written and shared in Scripture and, in particular, the gospels. It is in the life of Jesus as witnessed in the gospels that we discover the truest reflection of presence and pastoral ministry.

Here I have focused on two biblical stories to help elucidate the meaning of presence today for chaplaincy within education. First, I will consider the example of Eli and Samuel (1 Samuel 3:2–15), where we read about Samuel's journey to understand God's presence in his life.

This account recalls not just 'the breakthrough moment' regarding Samuel's faith but also the struggle of uncertainty. It is this struggle that is commonplace for all people who seek to understand God in their lives. This biblical account reflects the journey of many young people today.

In the research reported in *Religion and Education,* many young people experience God as 'a friend', or as somebody who has 'a plan for my life'. However, many of the respondents struggled with an association to the religious institution of their faith.[22] Taking the story of Eli and Samuel

20 Kevin Adams, 'Defining And Operationalizing Chaplain Presence: A Review', in *Journal Of Religion And Health*, 58.4 (2018), 1253.
21 Thomas G. Grenham, *Pastoral Ministry for Today*, Dublin: Veritas Publications, 2009, 40.

we observe a journey of indecision and confusion. In this scenario, we observe that instead of answering questions with prepared answers, Eli listens and accompanies Samuel on this journey. Eli, through this patient and enduring dialogue, has offered an example for chaplains and others accompanying young people today. Eli offers us the insight of a pastoral journey that understands that God is always involved in our lives as he goes before us in this life. He offers us an understanding of what it means not to be a protagonist in ministry but to be of service to ministry: *Speak, Lord, your servant is listening.*

Religious practice can often be misunderstood as a blind allegiance, or an unshakeable belief in a truth rather than a pilgrimage within life's journey. In the reality of today, religion for many young people offers more questions than answers. As a Church we are called to accompany our young people on this journey. This accompaniment is not a simple task of answering questions but is a lifelong journey of helping people to discover God's constant interjections in life. As former Archbishop Diarmuid Martin stated in an address to the National Religious Education Congress in 2013,

> … religious education is a lifelong project. Today, we have a heightened awareness that the religious education that is received in school will – no matter what its quality – never be sufficient for an adult to live his or her life faithfully in the complex world of today. It is a dialogue between faith and the realities of the world which responds to the real challenges of modern life in Ireland and helps the Christian to live the realities of his or her faith in a mature way in a changing society.[23]

The second biblical example is from the New Testament and recounts the post-resurrection world on the road to Emmaus (Luke 24:13–35). At the Synod on Young People Pope Francis used the Emmaus Story to

22 Gareth Byrne and Leslie J. Francis, op. cit., 133.
23 Sarah MacDonald, 'Religious education is a lifelong project – Archbishop', CatholicIreland.net, www.catholicireland.net/religious-education-lifelong-project-archbishop-martin/ (accessed 16 May 2021).

model a way of how to be involved in ministry and mission today. In this gospel scene, Jesus asked the two followers to share the story of their times. Jesus' approach was empathetic and engaging. As we contemplate the Emmaus story, we understand that Jesus did not dismiss the disciples' experience but entered the experience with them as he accompanied them on the road. Also important in this story is that Jesus did not ask the two to stop and return to Jerusalem but instead walked with them away from the city. Jesus, through this example, offers a true example of accompaniment today.

Later, and only after the invitation to stay, Jesus deepened the relationship with both disciples by 'breaking bread' with them. The two followers then came to a moment of transformation and realisation. 'Were not our hearts burning within us while he talked with us on the road and opened the Scriptures to us' (Luke 24:32)? They were changed and missioned through this experience to share the Good News. They returned to Jerusalem, the scene of a most difficult life experience, to share this new perspective that gives 'fullness of life'.[24]

Both biblical examples offer us the foundation of a model for chaplaincy that can respond effectively to our times. The recently published *New Directory of Catechesis* (DC) emphasises the approach of accompaniment: 'The whole of the DC hinges on understanding and appreciating the connection between catechesis and evangelization, and the vital role of accompaniment in both.'[25]

Accompaniment is a faith presence and a practice that is essential for today's chaplains and those they serve. Accompaniment is an expression of solidarity with people and a practice that reflects the ministry of Jesus as witnessed in the gospels.

Gospel Job Description for Chaplaincy

The chaplain in a faith-based educational community cannot be an

24 John 10:10.
25 Matthew Halbach, *The New Directory for Catechesis: Highlights and Summaries for Catechists and Pastoral Leaders*, Mystic, CT: Twenty-Third Publications (Kindle edition), 6.

added extra to its foundational mission. The chaplain accompanies young people, through a lens of faith, in an ever-changing community and culture. The chaplain offers young people solidarity in times of joy, anxiety, celebration and sadness.

The context for educational communities and chaplains is ever changing. Many contemporary educational communities can be considered parochial, yet for many they are disconnected from their past. They are open and welcoming communities but populated by many young people living in virtual worlds where their identities are constantly in transition. Pope Francis calls all involved in pastoral service to young people to create a dynamic Church of the people. A Church that walks with people and recognises that young people are the 'now of God',[26] not just the future of a world yet to be revealed.

Saint Pope John Paul II's address to the World Youth Day in the Philippines (1995)[27] had the theme: 'As the Father has sent me, so am I sending you' (John 20:21). So, what does this mean today? It points to the understanding that it is Christ who sends. The chaplain's identity and presence are embedded in the life and ministry of Jesus as shared with us in the gospels. Chaplaincy needs to be rooted in the example of Christ, and we should be trying not only to believe as Jesus believed but to live as Jesus lived.[28]

The chaplain has many qualities but the following 'biblical characteristics' can be considered important as part of any pastoral response to today's world.

1. Chaplains should create **healthy relationships** with all they encounter. Christian community is a central component in creating a safe space for people to be their authentic self. Jesus invited people into community. They accepted this invitation because he had something radically different to offer to the culture of his

26 Pope Francis, World Youth Day Homily, 2019.
27 Pope John Paul II, 'Address of His Holiness John Paul II to the Young People in "Rizal Park", www.vatican.va/content/john-paul-ii/en/speeches/1995/january/documents/hf_jp-ii_spe_19950114_vigilia-manila-gmg.html.
28 Michel de Verteuil, 'Believing as Jesus Believed', VICS, 2004.

day. The four gospels are littered with examples of Jesus meeting with people in different contexts. In each of these contexts Jesus created healthy and life-giving relationships. The fundamental key skill of any chaplain is the development of relationships.

2. The chaplain's **starting point for ministry is the context of life itself**. In many gospel scenes Jesus meets people at a time where life is difficult. In the post-resurrection scene in John's Gospel, Jesus meets the disciples who are working as fishermen. His initial response to the disciples is not a judgemental query about their quick return to fishing. Instead of judgement, Jesus invites them to have breakfast. It is such a human act of generosity and kindness to people who were working all night. Jesus engaged with people's lives and invites us all to do the same.

3. The chaplain **recognises the beauty and complexity of each person**. A central understanding of our faith is that we are all made in the 'image and likeness of God'. St Irenaeus put it best: 'The Glory of God is a person fully alive.' The chaplain should endeavour to bring this understanding of life alive for all.

4. Ministering as a chaplain with people implies that **the means of doing something is as important as the task itself**. In the story of the road to Emmaus, Jesus did not decide to cut short the process of walking with the disciples. He deliberately stayed with the two pilgrims until it was time to leave. Today, many young people are seeking new ways to participate and engage with the communities in which they live. These new ways will be discovered only if we share the road with them.

5. Being connected to young people through chaplaincy means being **open to the reality of young people and how that might change us**. In the story of Lazarus (John 11:1–44) Jesus arrived in the context of grief and loss. Jesus was moved by the loss and 'wept'. As chaplains we are asked to be open and vulnerable to the context we serve.

6. **Connecting to the 'whole' person, not just the spiritual**, is a core element of a chaplain's ministry. In Matthew 14:13–21, we learn from the scene where Jesus feeds the five thousand after having ministered to them. Jesus was not satisfied with healing people alone. He wanted to ensure all were physically fed as well as healed.

7. Chaplains are invited to **reach out to all those who are not currently engaged by existing ministries**. Jesus' ministry was not just to the religious Jewish people but to those on the margins. In the parable of the Pharisee and the tax collector (Luke 18:9–14), we are told that this parable was shared with those 'who were confident of their own righteousness and looked down on everyone else' (Luke 18:14). In this scene, Jesus spoke directly to the orthodoxy of the day, but he also invited people on the margins to be part of the kingdom of God. As chaplains we are also invited to share this mission of Jesus.

Conclusion

Religious educationalist Thomas Groome described Catholic education in the following terms: 'Catholic education intends to inform and form the very "being" of its students; Catholic education aims not only to influence what students know and can do but also the kind of people they will become.'[29] This is true, not only of Catholic education but of all denominational education. Faith-based education is interested in the development of the young people it serves. Central to this mission is the role of chaplaincy. Unfortunately, in many voluntary educational communities throughout Ireland, there are no chaplains. Each educational community within this sector today is expected to fund its own chaplaincy service through its own resources (personnel or financial). Resources from outside agencies (government or religious bodies) are limited or not available for many reasons. Where this lacuna exists in the delivery of

---

29 Thomas Groome, *The Contemporary Catholic School: Context, Identity and Diversity*, New York, NY: Routledge, 1996, 107–125, at 121.

the educational mission, it needs to be addressed as a matter of urgency for today's context.

Pope Saint John Paul II spoke these words when talking to people in leadership and youth ministry during his visit to the Philippines:

> In the course of their journey young people look for someone who … will know how to speak to their hearts and enkindle, comfort and inspire enthusiasm in them with the joy of the Gospel and the strength of the Eucharist … will know how to speak to them about the problems which worry them, and propose solutions, values, perspectives which are worth staking one's future on.[30]

The chaplain within an educational setting is the embodiment of John Paul II's vision. Chaplaincy is a ministry to a community that expresses a lived pastoral understanding of Jesus' earthly ministry and a commitment to Jesus' commandment: 'Just as I have loved you, you also should love one another. By this everyone will know that you are my disciples.'[31] Chaplaincy is a core structure within an educational community, which is at the service of the educational mission. It is a person-centred, value-led response on behalf of the educational community. To borrow Gustavo Gutiérrez's phrase in relation to Latin-American liberation, chaplaincy is 'ultimately about God'.[32]

30 Pope John Paul II, 'Address of His Holiness John Paul II to the Students and Representatives of the University of 'Santo Tomás', www.vatican.va/content/john-paul-ii/en/speeches/1995/january/documents/hf_jp-ii_spe_19950113_address-to-st-thomas-university.html.

31 John 13:34–35.

32 Daniel G. Groody, *Modern Spiritual Master Series, Gustavo Gutiérrez Spiritual Writings*, Robert Ellsberg (ed.), Maryknoll, NY: Orbis Books, 2011, 25.

7: A Light in the Darkness: Practical Theology and the Practice of Chaplaincy

Thomas G. Grenham

'Our Christian tradition takes the physical world and the multiplicity of peoples seriously, claiming that God's revelation can come to us at any time and place, through any culture, any society, and any person. Christians, therefore, have no business identifying only the bad and inferior in cultures, but must actively look for signs of God's presence.'
Anthony J. Gittins[1]

This chapter is about how chaplains interpret the Christian story and vision in order to provide life-giving meaning to the lived human story and vision. I wrote this piece when the Covid-19 pandemic was at its height. At this time, I experienced the tragic death of a family member and, as one who was bereaved, I experienced at first hand the ministry of hope offered by chaplains. They interpret God's revelation in practical ways so that God is made present in people's lives, a God who is very much present, active and powerful in the fragility, vulnerability and limitation of our human condition. I am reminded of St Paul and his claim that his strength came from his weaknesses. We have been reminded again during the Covid-19 pandemic of how fragile life is and how vulnerable we all are in the face of uncertainty. Awakening to this vulnerability and seeing it as a strength is a gift. St Paul was keenly aware of his own fragility when he claimed, 'For it is when I am weak that I am strong' (2 Corinthians 12:10). Paul saw strength in vulnerability and limitation.

Chaplains facilitate the discovery of life-giving meaning in their

---

1   Anthony J. Gittins, *Reading the Clouds: Mission Spirituality for New Times*, Barnhart, MO: Liguori Press, 1999, 165.

encounters with people who experience both joy and sadness throughout their lives. They are a light in the darkness. During the harrowing time of uncertainty and fear during the unprecedented pandemic challenge, chaplains have been busy offering their services of supportive and reassuring presence. In some cases, and in contexts where it is safe, they offer a cautious and socially distanced face-to-face presence, but intensive online support is also offered.

What does the chaplain 'do'? Who *is* the chaplain? Where does the chaplain belong? Are significant questions we might explore. Many people need spiritual support and reassurance that there is meaning and purpose to their lives in the midst of the Covid-19 pandemic, among other difficult events and tough life experiences. Chaplains are also present and available for happier times, marking special celebrations and seasonal liturgical events. From a Christian faith perspective, the chaplain, in various ways, is a representation of God's presence in human affairs, whether people are practising their faith or not. Alan Baker writes that 'Core to the chaplain is a commission to bear the image of God, despite your own obvious imperfections and brokenness, to the faces and hearts of those who otherwise may never enter a house of worship except for a wedding or a funeral.'[2]

Bearing the Image of God

It is fair to say we all carry a particular image of who God is for us and how God is present and active in our lives. Sometimes we call this an 'operative theology', whereby we have learned from our families and communities of faith a theology that we believe in and live by every day. It may be a very simple understanding of God's presence in our lives. We are familiar with phrases such as the 'man above', or 'the man upstairs', or 'it's the will of God', or 'God looking down on us', or 'only God knows', or 'with God's help' and so on. These sayings reflect a particular

---

2   Alan T. Baker, *Foundations of Chaplaincy: A Practical Guide*, Grand Rapids, MI: William B. Eerdmans Publishing Company, 2021,1–2.

image of what God is like for people. The image of God we inherited, or that we are influenced by, changes as time moves on, as new experiences of the world impact upon us, and as we get older. God does not change. Our image of who God really is, and how God is present and how God acts, develops and matures within the context of our lived experiences. For some, the image of God might be a threatening figure, 'watching', ready to mete out punishment for wrongdoing. For some, God is not a loving God, but an intimidating God, a policeman with punitive authority.

What most often challenges our image of God is when we experience difficulties, challenges, tragedies, suffering and the death of loved ones. On the one hand, trying to see and believe in a loving and compassionate God in the midst of suffering is hard for all believers. Yet, on the other hand, our image of God can be influenced by love, empathy, compassion and inclusion in the ebb and flow of our daily lives. It is easier to see a loving, understanding and forgiving God when things are going well for us … It is another story when inexplicable tragedy comes to our door. Our faith is often challenged when we experience deep suffering, which can spark a feeling of emptiness and a sense of meaninglessness and lack of purpose in our lives. For example, it is sometimes very difficult to believe that God is really present to us and walking with us in our suffering, especially when in the throes of serious illness.

For Christians, the clearest image of a loving and caring God is reflected in the life, death and resurrection of Jesus. Jesus' life, and particularly his ministry, revealed an image of God that is significantly connected with the ongoing encounters and fragility of human affairs. God coming into the world as a defenceless little infant in humble surroundings and a context of social deprivation, represented by the manger in Bethlehem, teaches us about a God who is interested in the vulnerability and the fulfilment of every human person. Such a birth teaches us something about a God who is present and active in the direst of situations. The incarnation of God in a human person like Jesus offers hope to a fragmented, broken and suffering world. Among many tasks and duties, helping people to grasp that image and the hope that God offers is the function of the chaplain.[3]

The Role of the Chaplain

In the past chaplains were mostly ordained priests. They administered the sacraments, especially when one was close to death. This form of chaplaincy was generally referred to as a sacramental model of pastoral care. Chaplaincy was mostly required at the hour of death, usually to administer *viaticum,* meaning 'provision for a journey', familiarly known as 'the last rites'. The dying person would receive communion, if they were able, and be anointed. The clergy chaplains celebrated Mass at a particular time in hospitals, military barracks, schools, parishes and so on, and would administer holy communion.

Before the Second Vatican Council the theology of chaplaincy was to interpret the presence and action of God as being somehow mediated through the clergy to the faithful. The council was a watershed moment for the Catholic Church. It brought enormous change to how the Church would function in the modern world. One of these changes involved the role of the faithful, or the non-ordained laity. The laity would have a much more prominent role in the function of the institutional Church and the community of believers. The council also emphasised the importance of reading the signs of the times and responding to these signs with relevant meaning, life-giving purpose and realistic hope for all.[4] It is not easy studying the signs that might present themselves to us. Practical theologian Terry Veling says:

> To read the signs of the times is one of the most difficult theological tasks, yet it is a theological imperative. Too often

3   See Thomas G. Grenham, 'The Intercultural Reality of Pastoral Presence', in Thomas G. Grenham (ed.), *Pastoral Ministry for Today – 'Who Do You Say That I Am? Conference Papers 2008*, Dublin, Veritas Publications, 55ff.
4   Austin Flannery (ed.), *Vatican Council II: The Conciliar and Post-Conciliar Documents*, New York, NY: Costello Publishing Company (rev. ed.),1992, 905. The document on the *Pastoral Constitution of the Church in the Modern World* (*Gaudium et Spes*) states that 'At all times the Church carries the responsibility of reading the signs of the times and of interpreting them in the light of the Gospel, if it is to carry out its task.'

we do not behold the announcement of God in our present reality. Rather, we cling to what we already know of God, to tired and weary theological frameworks that have lost sense of timeliness, to religious truths that lull us to sleep rather than provoke us to wakefulness.[5]

Chaplains attend to God's presence and action in the lived human experiences of others. The current pandemic is a challenge to chaplains to attend to God's presence in such a 'sign of our times'. As James and Evelyn Whitehead note:

> The religious leader today is seen less exclusively as the one who *brings* God and more as one who helps *discern* God already present. The minister is a skilful attendant to the movements of God wherever these appear.[6]

In order to do that, chaplains need training and formation in various disciplines such as theology, psychology, anthropology, spirituality and counselling. They need good relational skills, such as listening, asking appropriate open-ended questions and being appropriately dispositioned in their presence to people who require their services. Chaplaincy studies are essential in developing and sustaining effective chaplains, both ordained and non-ordained, so that chaplaincy services are fit for purpose in reading the signs of God's infinite unconditional loving presence.

Chaplaincy Studies

The need for study for the professional role of chaplaincy is well recognised. An MA in chaplaincy studies and pastoral work offered at Dublin City University (DCU) is testament to the growing desire for an interdisciplinary approach to supporting and accompanying people on their life journey. Understanding various types of spirituality and having a good comprehension of Christian theology and spirituality is vital in a

---

5   Terry A.Veling, *Practical Theology: 'On Earth as It Is in Heaven'*, Maryknoll, NY: Orbis Books, 2005, 17.
6   James D. Whitehead and Evelyn Eaton Whitehead, *Method in Ministry: Theological Reflection and Christian Ministry*, Kansas City, MO: Sheed & Ward, 1995, 68.

religiously and culturally diverse society. Chaplaincy has generally been concerned with religious traditions, particularly Christian traditions. However, there is a growing need to look after those of no particular religious tradition and those who have lapsed in their practice of Christian faith. Christian believers are living among various belief systems of both a secular and religious nature.

At DCU I have the privilege to be involved in the training and formation of chaplains and pastoral workers who work in various pastoral contexts. One of the core understandings of chaplaincy is to learn how God is present in the chaplain no matter what the chaplain's belief system reflects. Effective chaplains have a capacity for being present to those who may be living by a religious or secular story and vision or, indeed, both at the same time. God is present in all contexts. We may not always know how God is present and active in various religious and secular traditions and contexts. For Christians, God is known through Jesus the Christ of faith.

God's Presence and Action Personified in the Christian Chaplain

Practical theology, the science of God's revelation, presence and action, is very much impacted by what happens in the historical, social, political, religious and economic contexts anywhere on the planet. The reality of who God is becomes revealed to us in the dynamic dialectic conversation between the lived experience of humanity and the revelation contained in the biblical texts. The personhood of the chaplain serves the purpose of helping in that revelation, accompanying and supporting those who search for meaning and purpose in that dynamic conversation between their lived experiences and the experiences contained in the biblical tradition, particularly the gospels. Chaplains are specifically called to do this work of being with people in their particular lived contexts of joy, sadness, despair, suffering, expectation, anticipation, happiness and so on. The insightful chaplain discovers that the constants of faith, truth, love, justice, compassion, forgiveness, suffering, and life and death exist in every context. Alan Baker notes that

> God is the strength of chaplaincy because it takes God's
> specific calling to want to serve beyond the walls of a house
> of worship. If you sense your feet leading you toward people
> where they work, play, suffer, heal, laugh, cry, and even die,
> then chaplaincy is worth your consideration.[7]

Dealing with Religious Certainties and Cultural Bias

No one is born with prejudices. These are learned ways of behaviour
and received attitudes that are passed on through the generations of
cultural heritage and formation. The chaplain is not immune to bias.
Much healing can happen if the philosophy or the theology of presence
is incorporated into a meaningful and appropriate pastoral relationship.
However, sometimes our own religious certainties and cultural biases can
block that inner freedom to allow God be God in our lives.

The sense that my faith perspective is unsurpassed may be an
unconscious attitude. The perception that my own cultural world-view is
the most congenial, beneficial, life-giving and meaningful for my life, and
perhaps for the lives of others, could influence the way I engage those who
are 'different'. If it works for me, you should believe it, embrace it, select it
and belong to it! How many of us believe this unconsciously? On various
occasions the historical Jesus confronted different people and challenged
their assumptions about themselves. He particularly confronted their
prejudices in relation to their practised religious tradition and world-view.

During his time, the Pharisees, lawyers and Sadducees had their
comfort zones challenged by Jesus' encounter with them. However, they
chose not to change because of their own bias for power, privilege and
status. They were afraid to let go of a life-restricting image of themselves
because of a fear of loss of their culturally and religiously established
sense of identity within the community. It seems to me that prerequisites
for being an authentic pastoral agent with an effective presence are an

7   Alan T. Baker, op. cit., 2.

ability to open oneself to learning and growing and the possibility for personal transformation that occurs when we enter the space of another. Henri Nouwen often spoke of our agency as 'wounded to the wounded'.[8] Our patients, our parishioners, our marginalised, our unemployed, our refugees, our prisoners and others in need make manifest to us the loving presence of God, and they become our most profound teachers in inviting us to a deeper understanding of ourselves and the meaning of our vocation to ministry. We can be changed and transformed by those who die, those who suffer grievously, those who feel disillusioned, those who have lost hope and those who struggle on the margins of society. Yet, through all their suffering, there is a willingness to transcend the current painful reality and inspire others, including the minister. Suffering humanity has so much to teach us about life and its abundance. A theology of life-giving presence is helpful to understand how God is present to us and is with us in this constant human struggle to live a life of fulfilment, freedom and wisdom. Such a practical theological vision is interpersonal, intercultural and interreligious.

An Intercultural Theology of Presence

From a Christian theological and spiritual perspective, it is a ministry of presence that reflects God's love and action in the world of human relationships. For Christians, such a presence is embodied in the life and ministry of the historical Jesus, who became for the world the Christ of faith.

I suggest that the genuine sharing of God's love, i.e. the unconditional and incarnational love revealed contextually by the historical Jesus, is an intercultural, interpersonal, conversational dynamic between all cultures: religious and non-religious. For Christians, the seeds of God's love,

8 Henri J. M. Nouwen. *The Wounded Healer: Ministry in Contemporary Society*, Garden City, NY: Image Books, 1979. Nouwen contends that 'ministers are called to recognise the sufferings of their time in their own hearts and make that recognition the starting point of their service.' For Nouwen, 'ministers must be willing to go beyond their professional role and leave themselves open – as fellow human beings with the same wounds and suffering – in the image of Christ.'

preached and embodied by the historical Jesus, who became the Christ of faith, exist in all cultures and religious perspectives. The pastoral task is to discover and observe manifestations of God's vision or realm within every culture and religion. For example, for Muslims, God's (Allah's) dominion is everywhere and is revealed through the prophet Mohammed (Peace Be upon Him). In the sacred Koran God (Allah) speaks of a dominion of peace, love and dignity for all. Likewise, within the other religions of the world, the passion for transcendence, life, truth, friendship and meaningful belonging are reflected for humanity in different ways.

God's agenda for humankind is unconditional love, forgiveness and life-giving inclusive belonging. In various ways different cultures and religions reflect this agenda. The evolving religious constructions of meaning handed down from generation to generation engage the temporal and spiritual characteristics of human life in its struggle to find worthwhile meaning and purpose. These meaning constructions are embodied in symbols – persons, texts, sacraments, institutions, rituals, creeds and so on – and give shape to a life-giving pastoral presence. For Christians the cross is a powerful symbol of God's suffering presence. It is a reminder to us that God holds us and loves us in our suffering turmoil and is in faithful solidarity with us through every inch of our suffering. It does not end there. During Easter our Christian tradition celebrates the resurrection that follows the cross. We believe that we will rise again and live forever. Our liturgies have the potential to help us construct life-giving meaning and to reflect and make visible the presence of God. Simply lighting a candle in a church can connect us to something greater than ourselves. Such meaning constructions enable people to communicate, educate and form significant perceptions of themselves as loved. Furthermore, these actions shape an understanding of an ultimate reality such as God. For Christians, the significance and purpose of life, understood in the context of the Reign of God proclaimed by Jesus, provides a powerful foundation for hope in the face of suffering, illness and death. For others, different symbols and foundations of hope will connect them to the transcendent and to the meaning of their suffering and their joy.

My own theology of ministry is grounded in the metaphor of incarnation. God empathised so much with our humanness that God became one like us. God wanted to be so present to us that this presence became concretised and symbolised in the historical Jesus who became the Christ of faith. Some practitioners of ministry may want to use the language of the Trinity as another helpful way to understand the relationality of ministry. Highlighting the importance of relationship as the receptacle for human transformation, John Patton observes that

> Rediscovering one's self and one's power to live and to change
> in the context of relationship is what pastoral care is all about.
> Care is pastoral when it looks deeper than the immediate
> circumstances of a person's life and reminds that person that
> he or she is a child of God created in and for relationship.[9]

Assisting people in coming to understand that they are children of God may be difficult, especially when the suffering other is in a painful space. Do I, as a caregiver, have a sense that I am a child of God in my own ministry to the broken and fragile patients, clients and parishioners? What is my sense of incarnational theology? How is God made concrete in my own life? Whatever the answers to these questions are, I need to reflect a genuine embodiment (presence) and be a visible witness to the Christian faith I profess. The minister needs to walk the talk of Christian faith. Ministry is not an occasion for proselytising for a particular faith, especially to those who are most vulnerable because of loss, illness, relationship breakdown, imprisonment or bereavement. Should this happen then we create a hostage situation for the patient or family. This action would not reflect the God Jesus knew.

Jesus' Ministry of Care and Compassion

Jesus' ministry illustrated God's presence and action in the world of his time. This was service towards the reign of God. Jesus was a visible

---

9   John Patton, *Pastoral Care: An Essential Guide*, Nashville, TN: Abingdon Press, 2010, 30.

expression of the reign of God. He did not so much come to talk about himself as to help his listeners grasp the notion of God's reign: how this reign was shaped and where it could be found. Jesus' words and actions reveal the nature of God and the nature of Jesus' ministry. We get a glimpse of a God whose face is Jesus and whose face is also revealed in the people whom Jesus came to serve. This is a God who includes those who are marginalised by general society, a God who breaks down cultural and religious taboos, a God who heals people who are broken-hearted from relationships gone wrong, whose dreams have been dashed and who have lost hope in their own potential for life. The incarnation of God, in a human person like Jesus, offers hope to a fragmented and broken world. Helping people grasp that hope is a task for the pastoral agent. This was the very presence of God to the people around him and beyond. Jesus' ministry was the manifestation of the very presence and action of God.

Jesus' presence to various people and their presence to him provide us with a particular lens to explore our own sense of presence to those on the fringes of life. As the manifestation of God's presence, Jesus gave us the example of how to be visible expressions of God's presence through our ministry at this time of salvation history. See especially Luke 4:19–19 and Matthew 25:34–46, which powerfully reveal the specifics of God's reign. Jesus exuded a prevailing spiritual presence.

We interpret God's presence and action in our lives through the words and actions of Jesus in the gospels. Jesus healing the ten lepers, his Sermon on the Mount, his instructions to the disciples, his chastisement of the Pharisees and his storytelling in the parables all reveal a glimpse of the unconditional love and forgiveness of the God that Jesus knew. We are reminded of his presence on the cross and the type of presence that those under the cross were for him in his agony. This is what God is like, and the particular relationship that God envisioned for the world of humanity and the created environment. When Jesus withdrew to rest and pray, he was still present. We learn that to withdraw to pray and rest is also about establishing effective presence because we are always in relationship. Relationships have been established in our ministries. These relationships have to be nourished by prayer and rest in order for us to engage fully again and to enhance the quality of our ministry. Perhaps by our frequent prayer and reflection our intuitive sense of who God is for us and how God heals those around us can be sharpened. The culture we live in can offer glimpses of God as well as offer life-restricting characteristics of meaning-making. However, culture can be a communicative lens in which we can discover aspects of God's revelation and loving/saving presence among us.

In the Absence of Presence: The Terror of Meaninglessness

Theologians Patricia O'Connell Killen and John de Beer observe that 'For human beings the drive for meaning is stronger than the drive for physical survival. We need to make sense of what happens to us, to clothe our existence within an interpretative pattern that reflects back to us lives of integrity, coherence and significance. If we cannot, the will to live withers.'[10]

O'Connell Killen and de Beer highlight the need for meaning as the underpinning for our basic survival and that this meaning is uncovered through the interpretation of our experience in a particular context. To do this interpretation well, we need an appropriate, life-giving presence grounded in the wisdom of the responsible carer. Addressing the restrictions to life-giving meaning is important to allow a sense of personal freedom and wisdom to filter into the deepest recesses of a person's spirit. These obstructions are manifested in all kinds of ways, such as negative personal experiences reflected through painful relationships, hurtful events and abusive situations. Such blocks can be fearful.

The absence of a life-giving presence on the part of a pastoral agent gives rise to such experiences as spiritual terror, emotional isolation, relational separation or disconnection from the world of meaningful

10 Patricia O'Connell Killen and John De Beer, *The Art of Theological Reflection*, New York, NY: Crossroad Publishing Company, 1994, 1997, 45.

belonging, as well as other experiences of alienation, exclusion and loneliness. A patient or client who experiences a pastoral agent who is not fully present to them or seems distracted may feel discounted, stigmatised, unimportant, shamed or even bullied.

We are called to attend – to pay attention to what is happening around us. We are not called as ministers/chaplains to solve all problems for everyone. We are not present to 'fix'. Rather, we are present and available to others in order to support, empathise and stand in solidarity with them in their own struggles and help them discover for themselves solutions and 'answers' to what may be happening to them in their lives. It is about promoting, advocating and fostering a life-giving and safe space to grow, to heal, to transform, and to live and to die with dignity. Creating a life-giving space for healing and transformation is, as Bob Whiteside observes, ' … the task of those called to pastor, whether as youth ministers, pastoral workers, priests etc., to create and maintain such a space – a compassionate space where people can enter in, be held, restored and transformed as they face the numerous issues in their lives'.[11] For this compassionate space to be fostered the pastoral carer needs a secure, genuine, authentic pastoral identity. This is important and vital.

Shaping a Pastoral Identity

When Jesus asked that question of his disciples, 'Who do you say that I am?', he may have indicated that he needed some clue as to the meaning of his own presence among them and the reason for his ministry. Or he may have been testing the disciples to see if they had a sense of his pastoral identity and a sense of their own purpose as pastoral agents. It was in the conversation with them that clarity around Jesus' identity emerged. Peter responded with the insight, 'You are the Messiah'. A sense of personal and pastoral identity seemed to undergird Jesus' question. The answers he received when he asked the question first time around

11   See Bob Whiteside, 'The Art of Pastoral Ministry', in *The Furrow*, Vol. 59, No. 7/8 (2008), 399.

could have confused his identity with other known prophets until Peter clarified precisely who Jesus was: a saviour or liberator for their world.

John Patton suggests that

> Identity has been defined as the very 'core' of a person towards which everything else is ordered. It is something that, if one knows it, provides the 'clue' to a person. Identity is the specific uniqueness of a person, what really counts about him, quite apart from both comparison and contrast to others.[12]

In relation to shaping a secure and integrated pastoral identity, I am reminded of when the opposite was the reality in my own formation and training as a pastoral minister and chaplain in a large American hospital. During my Clinical Pastoral Education (CPE) formation, I had the experience of what is called in a United States hospital a code 99 emergency. My beeper went off and immediately I went to the relevant ward to discover that the patient was being attended to in a very urgent way. He was surrounded by medical staff who were anxiously caring for him. No part of his body was visible. In that moment, I wondered what need there was for me. What I had to offer was of little use in this extreme emergency, or so I thought. To further add to my doubts, the nurse on the ward called out in a loud, elevated voice that all non-essential personnel should leave the room ... she was looking at me. As I left the ward, I was full of doubt about whether or not I was really needed and wondered about how important non-medical people really are in these situations? After all, the chaplain or minister has few 'tools' and skills to help people in these emergencies. What can a chaplain 'do'? Over time, I did learn how to be a significant, non-anxious healing presence in such circumstances for the clinical staff, patients and families. I learned that my presence as a chaplain made a unique and essential contribution as a source of spiritual and emotional support and comfort, as advocate and healer for the community involved in these extreme emergencies. My identity as a pastoral agent eventually became shaped by practice and

---

12   John Patton, op. cit., 26.

support from fellow colleagues in CPE and staff at the hospital. Some skills of communication were helpful in such extreme emergencies.

The next time I was able to be present in such situations and to pray for the patient and staff in the midst of the emergency without impeding the actions of the doctors and nurses. I was able to see that I was part of the 'healing' team and part of the culture of the hospital. I could feel a sense of identity as a priest chaplain and pastoral care worker.

Our culture, society and religious environments are significant components in shaping our identities as individual persons and communities. Identity is a relational, interpersonal process. Culture is everything that engages human beings in the living of their lives. The ideas we have about each other, our behaviour, the meaning we interpret from experience, our emotions, the material artefacts that we gather, the food we eat and the languages we speak all point to a cultural framework in which we live and have our essential being or existence. Such identity is further influenced by a plurality of cultures and religions that we encounter in our contemporary ministry. Effective chaplains stand in their religious traditions and are faithful to their beliefs, while at the same time they can be open and respectful of those of different belief systems and world-views.

Conclusion

Earlier, I mentioned St Paul and his claim to fame for embracing the strength of his weaknesses and I end this chapter with the full citation in Corinthians. This is such a key insight into practical theology and for the practitioners of chaplaincy services. Paul says to the Corinthians, 'My grace is enough for you: my power is at its best in weakness. So I shall be very happy to make my weaknesses my special boast so that the power of Christ may stay over me, and that is why I am quite content with my weaknesses, and insults, hardships, persecutions, and the agonies I go through for Christ's sake. For it is when I am weak that I am strong' (2 Corinthians 12:9–10).

The emotional and spiritual strength of the chaplain is the ability to embrace our own vulnerabilities, sufferings, losses and bereavements appropriately and see in them the power of God's presence and action. These 'weaknesses 'or 'flaws' will be the ingredients, managed appropriately, undergirding the chaplain's life-giving and hope-filled presence for others trying to find meaning in their lived experiences of joy and sadness. This is practical theology being practised at the coalface of everyday life.

8: Chaplaincy, Dialogue and Encounter: The Key to the Future

Alan Hilliard

'The worst thing that can happen to us is that we stay behind, looking in the mirror, dizzy from so much spinning around without an exit. To get out of the labyrinth we have to leave behind the 'selfie' culture and look at the eyes, faces, hands, and needs of those around us; and in this way find, too, our own faces, our own hands full of possibilities.'
Pope Francis and Austen Ivereigh[1]

Introduction

Chaplaincy in Ireland has changed. Until recently the narrative was one where a chaplain was appointed by a bishop or the superior of a religious order to minister in a specific setting. The organisation requesting the chaplain largely trusted the bishop or superior. A chaplain who was deemed appropriate and acceptable over a period of time in the post, was left there until required somewhere else or if he or she needed a change. Now things very are different, especially for chaplaincy roles that are publicly funded.

I recently negotiated a contract of service at TU Dublin for a multi-faith pastoral care and chaplaincy service via a public procurement process, and it is clear that the difference brings new and added processes, procedures and outcomes. The process has caused paradigm shifts of sorts that one would be foolish to ignore if religious bodies wish to stay in chaplaincy work in the future. There are a number of features in this shift from appointment to procurement that impact on chaplaincy. Firstly, those requesting the tender decide what elements of the service are to be

---

1 Pope Francis and Austen Ivereigh, *Let Us Dream*, New York, NY: Simon & Schuster (Kindle edition), 136–37.

provided. Secondly, the organisation providing the chaplaincy service, which in many cases is the diocese, is the one that is asked to engage more responsibly with the agency requiring the service (e.g. the hospital or university). This is no longer left to the individual chaplains as was the case in the past. Thirdly, the purpose of the contract is to create a value for service – the purchaser wants value for their money, which translates into performance indicators or KPIs. There is no room for legacy agreements, sense of entitlement or tardiness, as regular reviews examine all aspects of the contract to ensure that value for money is to the fore. Chaplains may feel they are doing the best job according to their own particular understanding of chaplaincy, or they may in the past have decided what an appropriate workload is – now they have to provide a service that is ultimately decided and outlined by those who pay! That dreaded word accountability has been introduced into the equation, and this can send chaplains into a downward spiral of feeling undervalued and untrusted. There are, of course, some chaplaincies funded by religious bursaries which may not have these recent challenges, but this is less and less the case. However, such chaplaincies have a moral obligation to ensure that resources are not being squandered and that the needs of those being served are to the fore.

Whatever an individual point of view, if faith-based organisations and individuals want to continue to be involved in chaplaincy, this is the present and it is most definitely the future. Some may feel undermined and undervalued by what one could term 'the metric society', and there is no doubt that there are some services, like chaplaincy, that are difficult to evaluate fully. Reflecting on this contemporary challenge in chaplaincy a business colleague said recently, 'It's like getting me to evaluate to a third party how good a dad I am.' This contemporary era brings new realities to providers of chaplaincy services. We could put our heads down and think that it will go away, but it won't. Another approach would be to see this as just another anti-Church attack by militant secularists, but it isn't. A third approach is to embrace the reality and the opportunities it presents.

The opportunities are challenging but this should not be daunting. There is an opportunity to provide training that highlights how committed and professional chaplains are while still emphasising that faith and belief is what motivates them to do the work of chaplaincy.

As in times past the Church today has to negotiate its place in society and in individual settings too. Too often we let the past be our present only to lose or compromise our future. The reality described in the opening paragraphs of this chapter, while presenting new challenges for pastoral care and chaplaincy services, is one of hope. Pope Francis encourages us to dream our way out of our present limitations in this period of our history. The fact that many are focusing on reductions in vocations to priesthood and religious life, the viability of some parishes and even the possibility of financial collapse is reason enough to consider a reconfiguration of the Church's activities. Maybe this is not the optimum time to be 'dreaming', but neither is it the time simply to give up or to become lethargic. This article takes on board the challenges that chaplaincy faces today and shows how these realities are in keeping with Pope Francis's strategy of dialogue and encounter, which underpins his invitation to us to dream together. This is a time for new thinking in the face of our changing environment and culture. According to Pope Francis, 'God asks us to dare to create something new. We cannot return to the false securities of the political and economic systems we had before the crisis.'[2]

In asking us to move in this direction he gives us the tools of dialogue and encounter, with which we can achieve our dreams. The Church has achieved its greatest outcomes when it approaches situations in a dialogical manner. An initial overview of the life and theology of Bernard Häring before looking at the characteristics of dialogue and encounter as found in Let Us Dream helps us to understand that dialogue and encounter in contemporary settings and with contemporary challenges are not new to the Church. These findings can be applied to the challenges facing chaplaincy today, both in individual settings – focused on those we

2   Pope Francis and Austen Ivereigh, op. cit., 6.

minister to – and in institutional settings. To be ministers of hope we must have hope!

Bernard Häring – A Lifetime of Dialogue

Bernard Häring was one of the foremost theologians of the Second Vatican Council. In 1948 his Redemptorist superior had a conversation with him that set his future in train. The superior was concerned about the number of priests who were appointed to Rome to study canon law. However, he was more concerned that on completion of their studies they were returning to seminaries and universities to teach moral theology. As a result of this meeting, where there was mutual agreement that morality was inappropriately dominated by law, Häring agreed to prepare a course to form people who would teach moral theology. Using the Word of God and social sciences the course opened with a module entitled 'Continuous Conversion As A Core Dynamic of Moral Theology'. When he started preparing his courses Häring discovered that he needed to adopt an ecumenical approach to his theological vision as resources among his Catholic colleagues were scarce. Subsequently his course was viewed with suspicion and the influential men in the Holy Office described his work as one that did not 'fit their notion of the Church'.[3] Häring remained on the periphery of the institutional Church until Pope John XXIII appointed him as a theological adviser to the Second Vatican Council. Though a wonderful academic, his theology was greatly influenced by his experience as a military chaplain in his early days of ministry.

As a chaplain during the Second World War Häring regularly disobeyed orders and ministered to the spiritual and humanitarian needs of soldiers on both sides of the battlefront and of civilians too. No doubt he was inspired in these actions by his mother. He remembered her kindness in his childhood when she welcomed those who were homeless and hungry after fighting in the First World War into their home. Sitting them at the

---

3   Bernard Häring, *My Hope for the Church, Critical Encouragement for the Twenty-First Century,* Alton, Hants: Redemptorist Publications, 1999, 13.

106

table she would always say, 'Today you are our guest'.[4]

When the war came to an end Häring was assigned to care for soldiers returning from battle and also for German refugees. He remembers preparing sixteen sermons to preach to his flocks. Once he set out on this mission he recalls that not one of his homilies made it to the pulpit! His time was spent listening to those he served and together they worked out 'a kind of morality that would try to respond to the burning experiences, hopes, and fears of our time'.[5] He also found that he had to develop a way of announcing the 'Good News' to reach the 'sort of person who had been sorely tried by life'.[6] His experience of his mother's goodness and his engagement with various groups via his ministry allowed dialogue to be the basis of his theological and prayerful reflections.

Dialogue was central to Häring's life and his theology, and dialogue is not an option for the Church. Rather, it is essential to the nature of the Church. In fact the Church ceases to be what Christ intended it to be if a dialogical approach is not adopted. The only reason people would shy away from this basic truth is if they are trying to hold on to 'their notion of the Church', which holds what they want and who they want in positions of power. Chaplaincy, as a mission of the Church, is therefore dialogical by its nature too.

Culture of Encounter

One could consider Häring's approach to his life, his faith and his theology as a precursor to what Pope Francis has termed a 'culture of encounter', of which dialogue is an essential component. Explaining the rationale behind this concept Archbishop Paul Gallagher, Secretary for Relations with States within the Holy See's Secretariat of State, said;

I think there is this spirit of pastoral renewal which [Pope Francis] has been trying to instil in the Church, by which within the Church and outside the Church many people feel

4   Ibid., 21.
5   Ibid., 9–10.
6   Ibid.

alienated from a very authoritarian, very dogmatic institution and he's sort of saying, No, let's put the people at the centre.[7]

Gallagher continued to outline that this encounter is essential for the promotion of a faith-based commitment and involvement with all levels of our society for the purposes of promoting the common good and to improve the life situations of people, especially the most vulnerable. We saw this in evidence in Haring's life and ministry. Furthermore, good relations are key to the culture of encounter, as 'you cannot dialogue with anyone you obviously disrespect or despise'.

To understand where this concept developed in Pope Francis's teaching Cardinal Michael Czerny, who works very closely with Francis and who is the Director of the Vatican's Dicastery for Migrants and Refugees, helps us understand the rationale of Pope Francis's promotion of the culture of encounter. He tells us that when Pope Francis was Archbishop of Buenos Aires he realised that his centre of gravity wasn't to be in the archiepiscopal office but in the slums and shanty towns surrounding the city.[8] As archbishop he made regular visits to these areas, travelling on the subways and trains, encountering the reality of people's lives and encountering his own belief and understanding in the process – this was not unlike Bernard Häring's work with refugees from the war. Czerny, I think, gives the best understanding of the culture of encounter in an interview with the BBC when he summarises it as a 'conversion of the feet'. Francis doesn't want any more 'isms' or institutions; he wants human beings to be respected and the world to 'behave its way out of this impasse'. Indeed, too much time can be wasted thinking and reflecting when so much has to be done!

One could ask what is dialogue and what is a culture of encounter in a chaplaincy context. One could even ask what is the difference between dialogue in the sense that Francis proposes and the useless, painful,

---

7   Ruth Gledhill, 'Archbishop Paul Gallagher explains the Pope's "Culture of Encounter"', *The Tablet*, www.thetablet.co.uk/news/8105/archbishop-gallagher-explains-the-pope-s-culture-of-encounter- (accessed 3 May 2021).
8   'A Culture of Encounter', BBC, www.bbc.co.uk/sounds/play/b09dxz1b (accessed 1 May 2021).

time-consuming ramblings that people or individuals can indulge in. A methodology that could answer these questions is proposed in *Let Us Dream,* an insightful study into Pope Francis's use of this dialogue and encounter methodology when facing personal issues and when discerning the right path on issues like poverty and the environment.

> Through many encounters, dialogues, and anecdotes like these my eyes were opened. It was like an awakening. In the night you see nothing, but little by little dawn breaks and you see the day.[9]

If we are looking for a guide to direct our energy and indeed our feet in the direction of People Francis's culture of encounter it is to be found in *Let Us Dream.* The book gives us methodology in its layout; to see, to choose and to act but, more importantly, throughout it gives us a deeper insight into the overall aim, workings and justifications for Francis's culture of encounter. This methodology can lead into the dynamic and active hope that chaplaincy provides. It can also help us to look at how our institutional Church can plan for chaplaincy into the future.

Religious Monologues

Maybe it is his age or maybe it's years of tiring meetings with few outcomes that have helped Pope Francis to develop a process that focuses on outcomes or, as Czerny calls it, 'conversion of the feet'. Whereas dialogue is necessary in the process of encounter it is not the end result – there is too much at stake and the end result has to be action. In his preparation for the document *Laudato Si'* Francis describes dialoguing with experts. He convened theologians and scientists and got them to put their heads together until they reached a synthesis in preparation for *Laudato Si'*.[10] However, he also describes dialoguing with fishermen in seaports around fishing villages in Italy. In the town of San Benedetto del Tronto he listened to one fisherman describe how they fish twelve tons of plastic out of the ocean each year, which they separate and bring to shore rather than throwing it back into the ocean.

9   Pope Francis and Austen Ivereigh, op. cit., 31.
10   Ibid., 32.

Focusing on outcomes preserves the integrity of the mission of the organisation and the Kingdom of God. David Tacey writes on the subject of how true mysticism is more a concern about the world than a concern about self. Quoting Merton he reminds us that mysticism 'is not and can never be a narcissistic dialogue of the ego with itself'.[11] In *The Postsecular Sacred* Tacey addresses the shortfall of established religions and their inability to address the situations they find themselves in today. He describes them as retreating into 'cocoons' of their own making, thus failing to be available to dialogue with the society of which they are a part. As a result they appear to be languishing, if not dead.

> If religious truth presents itself as fixed and absolute, unwilling to reinterpret itself for a new era, the 'old guard' will have their way and ensure that transformation does not occur.[12]

Dialogue

Not to adopt a proactive dialogical approach that focuses on outcomes and indicators within the mission and setting of chaplaincy can be detrimental to chaplaincy in any setting. We always have to be wary of the fact that our own need or ego can direct us towards a conscious or unconscious mission that will bring about the downfall of that to which one claims to be committed. A further insight helping us see the value of dialogue in our contemporary settings is that dialogue and encounter are 'congruent with our deepest nature'.[13] Scripture scholar Walter Brueggeman suggests that many of the problems with the decline of the churches in the West stems from their obsession with monologues.

> There can be no doubt that such a shrill voice of certitude, in any area of life, is an act of idolatry that is characteristically tinged with ideology.[14]

11   Thomas Merton, *New Seeds of Contemplation*, New York, NY: New Directions, 1961.
12   Tacey, David, *The Postsecular Sacred – Jung, Soul and Meaning in an Age of Change*, Abingdon: Taylor and Francis, 2019 (Kindle Edition), 15.
13   Walter Brueggemann, *Mandate to Difference – An Invitation to the Contemporary Church*, Louisville, KY: Westminster John Knox Press, 2007, 73.
14   Ibid., 74.

His justification for this stance comes from a reading of the Jewish critic George Steiner,[15] whose research claims that God is capable of all speech acts except those that are monologues. Both Brueggemann and Steiner refer to a number of scripture passages where Yahweh engaged with his representatives and new life-giving horizons opened for God's people. While Brueggeman promotes the need for a dialogical approach he does so not from a purely academic perspective, but out of his conviction that the Church has little option but to act and make a difference on behalf of those who are disenfranchised. He see that this 'anxiety-driven time provides an opportunity for dialogue that shows people the limits of our current economic, political and social systems'. The Christian community has no choice any more but to step out of dead monologues and embrace dialogues that are fostered by a culture of encounter. If we need to have it spelt out for us Brueggeman observes that 'the primary commitment of our culture to security, ideology, technology, certitude and community constitutes a system of hopelessness',[16] which is the antithesis of chaplaincy. If chaplaincy and the people of all faiths stay committed to monologues and remain quiet and isolated, 'the human spirit withers and options for newness grow jaded in fatigue'.[17]

To find a way forward one always needs a next step. In order to agree that dialogue and encounter are the next step we have to know how to get there. Considering the characteristic of dialogue and encounter in *Let Us Dream* will help us understand how to move towards a conversion of feet, which is the hoped-for outcome of the culture of encounter. So that we don't get lost in a slavish adherence to outcomes and activities, mirroring the sins of our neo-liberal age, we should remind ourselves of the motivation behind Pope Francis's pedagogy of 'a time to see, a time to choose and a time to act'. His wish is expressed in these opening lines:

> This is a moment to dream big, to rethink our priorities – what
> we value, what we want, what we seek – and to commit to act

15   See George Steiner, *Real Presences,* Chicago, IL: University of Chicago Press, 1989.
16   Walter Brueggemann, op. cit., 99.
17   Ibid., 94.

in our daily life on what we have dreamed of. What I hear at this moment is similar to what Isaiah hears God saying through him: Come, let us talk this over. Let us dare to dream.[18]

Dialogue in *Let Us Dream*

Dialogue is mentioned sixteen times in *Let Us Dream*. An overview of dialogue and encounter in the book reveals that dialogue is the toolbox of healthy and engaging encounters. An image used throughout the conversation is that of a river bursting its banks. The overflowing river does not bring hardship to river dwellers but provides a powerful image of new possibilities when hearts and minds meet in gracious and generous encounter and are opened up to one another.

> Such overflows of love happen, above all, at the crossroads of life, at moments of openness, fragility, and humility, when the ocean of His love bursts the dams of our self-sufficiency, and so allows for a new imagination of the possible.[19]

The word 'overflow', mentioned twenty-three times in this book, brings to mind the Eucharistic image of a cup overflowing and the utter generosity of God. It is as if the experience of this generosity is the outcome of mutual dialogue and encounter. Pope Francis personally attests to the fact that 'encounter, dialogue and anecdote' resulted in 'my eyes being opened'.[20]

Encounter and Dialogue

Speaking about the necessity of this pedagogy in today's culture Pope Francis admits that it is difficult to nurture encounter in what he terms the 'throwaway culture' that characterises our world today. For real and true encounter there has to be a mutual respect for one another, which is defined as 'shared dignity'. While we may enter a spirit of encounter with individuals and organisations we can often meet with an

18 Pope Francis and Austen Ivereigh, op. cit., 6.
19 Ibid., 81.
20 Ibid., 31.

'isolated conscience', which is an obstacle to promoting a shared and common vision. In this setting one encounters 'rigidity'. Whether one is a revolutionary or a restorationist, rigidity 'is a sign of the bad spirit concealing something'.[21]

For those involved in the negotiation for chaplaincy with public institutions many of these characteristics may be noticed. However, this is not enough reason to cease from pursuing meaningful encounters with those with whom negotiations are both necessary and advantageous. Chaplains in many settings, including prisons, hospitals and colleges, meet many such challenges regularly but they don't give up – nor should they. Those who are involved with negotiating contracts of service often find the encounters bewildering, but no matter how bewildering they are it is a journey towards engagement, dialogue and encounter, whereby there are benefits for all parties. Indeed, there can be a 'brimming over' for all parties when a common vision of the task is realised and the initial confusion and rigidity can be overcome.

Though these obstacles of rigidity or even misunderstanding or lack of literacy may win out or be to the fore at various times during dialogue, they can be overcome if we but hold on to the energy of Francis's vision for dialogue in a sincere culture of encounter. The overall purpose of encounter is to allow the Lord to open a new future for us where we thought there was none, or to recover a future that people were losing sight of.[22] No matter how extreme any crisis is, Pope Francis believes that recovery is the fruit of synthesis. The fusion of disparate elements can generate a whole that is greater than the sum of its parts. This truth is in evidence in Bernard Häring's ministry and theology.

Despite differences and difficulties remaining after encounters, disparate groups can share common goals and commit to creating a better future for the benefit of those they serve.[23] If we expect perfect outcomes or one-sided victories from dialogue then we misunderstand it.

21 Ibid., 69.
22 Ibid., 2.
23 Ibid., 100.

Rather, the space of encounter is a space of contemplation, which, Pope Francis admits, serves to provide an occasion to solve issues that cannot be fixed with complex norms. It is a space that provides an opportunity to encounter truth! It is an occasion to move from the safety of rigid thinking to explore the essence of the other with whom we dialogue and in so doing to reach into that space that gives us

> the trustworthy evidence that invites us to believe in them. Opening ourselves to this kind of certainty calls for humility in our own thinking, to leave space for this gentle encounter with the good, the true, and the beautiful.[24]

This experience reveals that ministry to the world cannot ignore the obstacles and challenges we come across in the depths of our own heart and soul and of our mission. While engaging with those to whom we minister and with the institutions within which we minister there is much that we need to take account of in any process of dialogue and discernment. However challenging or even painful this encounter is, averting our gaze so our eyes cannot see is not an option. What lies in this exchange is the seedbed of a new future. The very things that can appear as being in opposition may actually create the opportunity for a more refined understanding of the Church's mission in the world today. The best things don't come easy.

Conclusion

This chapter began by highlighting many of the contemporary challenges facing the varied situations of chaplaincy today. Changes occur that shift the setting and situation and requirements for the work of chaplains. We can be fearful of new settings and new contexts and this is precisely why this book is so helpful and timely. Whereas 'a time to see, a time to choose and a time to act' is the methodology of the book, the richness of this methodology lies in the nuances, its deeper processes and the openness to the 'other' as the dream is realised.

24   Ibid., 55.

Furthermore, the image of a river bursting its bank to refresh the land is one that is timely and needed. The aim of chaplaincy, in the context of the culture of encounter, is not to be right but to be open, to see distant horizons and to be hopeful that with the Gospel at the heart of their mission people can journey together towards their realisation, which is to serve those they are called to serve in a fulfilling and satisfying manner.

Chaplaincy today can remain fossilised in monologues of the past. If chaplaincy is to thrive then individuals and their sponsoring organisations have no option but to see beyond the pages of requirements and contracts. The right approach in this task, which can be guided by *encounter*, has every possibility of unveiling the real purpose and strength of the Church's missionary activity, not just in those who minister but in its administration of these activities. Chaplains are ministers of hope, but they must negotiate with hope and with the confidence that what they bring to any situation is an adherence to outcomes that create a more positive environment for human beings to flourish. While chaplains in former days may have avoided accountability, good supervision and performance management focused on desired outcomes may help the chaplain to remain focused, motivated, energised and hope-filled. Pope Francis's insights into dialogue and encounter throughout *Let Us Dream* provide a thought-provoking methodology and a rich, engaging process whereby these challenges can not only be met but can serve to create a vibrant ministry that can be infused with our hopes and dreams.

Part Three
Places of Hope

9: The Homeless

Susan Jones

*'God said, "Take off your sandals, for the place
where you are standing is holy ground."'*
Exodus 3:5

Complex Needs

Writing in *Jesus – Social Revolutionary?* Peter McVerry asks, 'Where is God to be found?'[1] One would not readily expect to find our God of love and compassion among those cast aside by their family or neighbours, people who are almost held captive by a homeless system, trapped in the tomb of stereotypical judgement as criminals or addicts. Well, if health and safety protocols [2] allowed me to walk around homeless hostels in my bare feet, I would, for it is on this sacred ground that I truly find God.

Providing chaplaincy services to men and women who experience homelessness and the staff[3] who work with them is truly humbling and life-giving. I often hear myself say, 'Lord, now I know why you came as you did.' While the basic skills and attributes are the same for all chaplaincies, you also need a sense of humour, a thick skin, a good head on your shoulders and strong professional boundaries. You have to know the values from which you operate, be confident in yourself and be honest about the social situation from which you come.[4] It is not a ministry for

---

1 Peter McVerry, *Jesus – Social Revolutionary?* Dublin: Veritas Publications, 2008, 46.
2 Needle-stick injuries are an ever-present risk, so covered footwear is essential for everyone.
3 The chaplain also ministers to the staff, keeping a caring eye on how they are impacted by events in the service, for example the death of a service user, changes within the organisation etc. A good rapport with staff is vital for the fulfilment of the chaplaincy role as staff can let chaplains know what is happening or what dynamics are at play among the service users.
4 See B. J. McClure, *Moving Beyond Individualism in Pastoral Care and Counselling: Reflections on Theory, Theology and Practice* [Online], 2008. Available from: The Lutterworth Press. https://ebookcentral.proquest.com/lib/itb/detail.action?docID=3433630 [accessed 29 April 2021], 227.

the timid or pious. The needs of those who are homeless are complex. Nothing is as straightforward as it seems. It is true that 'disadvantage in the broad sense is strongly implicated in homelessness',[5] but men and women from more affluent backgrounds are also homeless for the same reasons, albeit with differing nuances.[6] As McVerry reminds us, 'There is no difference between the deserving and undeserving poor.'[7] However, people coming from less disadvantaged communities do not have the social capital, community networks or social skills needed to cope with homelessness and hostel accommodation.

The First Night

Imagine arriving in a homeless hostel for the first time, having lost or left everything, with only what you hear in the media as your source of information about hostel life. As chaplain you need to share the hard truths of this reality with compassion, but most importantly talk about the love, camaraderie and support that is to be found here too. Life in a hostel is tough; you are not only coping with the fact that you have no home, very unstable accommodation (if you're in an emergency hostel), very limited personal space, sharing rooms with different people, no choice of meals or meal times if food is provided, nightly curfews, the risk of theft or violence, and, if you are not in addiction, the danger that you will give in to temptation.

Acceptance

Hostels can be a volatile place to be in ministry for you never know when something will kick off, but staff are usually at hand. Yet it is into this

5   A. Cleary, M. Corbett, M. Galvin and J. Wall, *Young Men on the Margins*, Dublin: Katherine Howard Foundation ISFC, 2004, 117.
6   Some of these differences might include gambling addiction rather than drugs. Some people might be hiding in homeless services for safety due to large outstanding debts to money-lenders. Relationship breakdown or domestic violence at any age is a factor for all, but some older men may present to homeless serves once their children are settled in life and they can step away from the emotional and mental abuse of their spouses. Lack of acceptance of sexual orientation among some communities has led to homelessness across all classes and some ethnic minorities.
7   Peter McVerry, op. cit., 29.

space that the Lord offers the grace-filled opportunities for the chaplain to enter 'more deeply into the mystery of a suffering God' and 'to point to the further truth of Christ risen and ascended behind the darkness'.[8] Following Christ's example of walking among those he served and listening to their needs, ministry in this environment is only possible when you see Christ fully embodied in those you serve. In upholding the person's dignity the chaplain 'formally embraces the person as embodied, gendered, and historicised, embracing the internal, external, and relational dimensions of [his or her] human personality.'[9]

As you find yourself sitting with homeless men and women on a kerbside, or at their bedsides in psychiatric, maternity and general hospitals, ER and ICU, or accompanying them to various appointments including GPs, sexual assault units, child access visits, various kinds of assessments and court visits or methadone clinics, you become privileged to hear life stories of struggle, trauma and enormous resilience.[10] The truths of these precious lives are told with joy, laughter, tears, anger or rage in the quiet of a dorm room or a busy smoke-filled smoking room. The men and women will notice how you respond or react for they are well clued in to the negative body language of ignorance or judgement. You don't know everyone's history. Sometimes, like a prison chaplain, you'll find yourself sitting with sex offenders, with someone who has raped another, or committed a violent crime, and at other times with people who have been traumatised as victims of such types of crimes. Then there are the times when, like hospital chaplains, you will sit with those diagnosed with a serious illness or be discussing treatment regimens for chronic illnesses. It is a really blessed experience when the men and women

8   P. Ballard and J. Pritchard, *Pastoral Theology in Action: Christian Thinking in the Service of Church and Society*, London: SPCK, 2006, 181.
9   E. Regan, *Theology and The Boundary Discourse of Human Rights*, Washington, DC: Georgetown University Press, 2010, 85.
10 As in other chaplaincies networking is important. Prison chaplains, hospital chaplains, homeless liaison workers, social workers, community welfare officers, Gardaí, along with agencies and organisations such as Rough Sleepers, Safetynet, Women's AID, Men's Aid, NALA, recovery centres, detox centres and counselling centres, among others, will be significant.

forget you are present as 'other' and carry on their banter with you in the middle. As chaplains we hold, by our unconditional acceptance, the truth before all truth, which is that we are all loved by the same understanding, non-judgemental God, and we must be open to receiving this same non-judgemental acceptance from those with whom we are in ministry with so that we can humbly serve.

It would be strange to talk about ministry in homeless services without mentioning substance addiction, particularly drugs. There is not much a chaplain can do pastorally when someone is very heavily under the influence. However, when a person in addiction is met with respect and compassion a trusting relationship can be established which opens up conversations about their addiction, sickness and debt, and you begin to understand the cross of addiction and the shackles of the 'liquid handcuffs'[11] of methadone.

Praying Together

Most homeless people are acutely aware of their 'status outside the community'[12] and do not feel they have any place in our Church. They feel unwelcome. (Yes, some go into a church in the winter to keep warm but they are usually asked to leave.) This does not mean they are not spiritual or have lost faith in God. Gathering with the people in hostels for prayer is a profoundly blessed time.

Hostels don't have quiet spaces to pray, so adaptability is key. It tends to be a space in the corner of the dining room or TV room that is used. We have gathered to pray on all key feast days, which contributes hugely to a sense of community.[13] I often reflect on these gatherings with a smile as

11 'Liquid handcuffs' is a term used by some in addiction to describe the loss of freedom that comes with being on a methadone programme in a clinic where you have to present every day to get your methadone. If you miss an appointment not only do you suffer physically, but alterations can be made to your allocated amount of methadone so your body suffers even more.
12 Cleary et al., op. cit., 126.
13 Mother's Day, Father's Day, St Brigid's Day (with the making and blessing of crosses), Ash Wednesday (for the distribution of ashes), Holy Week (with a service reflecting all the events at time of prayer), Easter Sunday, carol services and Christmas Day services. People will also ask for services for their own special times, like the anniversaries of children or parents.

the cuppa, or other stronger beverages, are usually brought along. Dinner might also be brought when I offer time to pray, sometimes met with the words, 'I don't think Jesus would mind.' With a great willingness to participate some residents volunteer to read, others roar out the words to help keen, struggling readers along,[14] and there can be many interruptions with, 'Oh, can we remember to pray for ... .' Talking during the service can sometimes lead to a row as others try to get silence. All contribute to the creative liturgical spontaneity that reflects the lives of those participating, yet a reverent respectfulness usually descends on the group. Somewhere within the internal chaos that homelessness brings the peace of God is glimpsed.

November remembrance services are highly significant. While there are deaths in the hostels, spouses or partners, children, family members and friends die. Unfortunately, babies are also miscarried or pregnancies terminated. Death can take down the defences and roll back any stones of bravado, exposing huge pain. It is in this space that solidarity and community break through. The sadness can be deeply tangible, so memorial services are genuinely significant. It is very difficult when a homeless person is not welcomed home to the funeral of a parent or sibling. Providing a prayer service at these times is a privilege as it enables the excluded person to say goodbye at some level. It is beautiful to witness the outpouring of support from others in the hostel who gather with the bereaved in their grief.

It is important to recognise the feast days and needs of other faith traditions (like Eid, or Chinese New Year) in our homeless hostels. The chaplain needs to advocate for prayer space and the provision of food before and after fasting during Ramadan, as well as encouraging the provision of food suitable for other religious believers.

---

14 See Cleary et al., op. cit., 121. Here Cleary discusses how lack of education among young men brings huge challenges and accordingly makes it hard to 'successfully transition from home to independent living'.

Finding Hope

Amid the struggle of homeless hostels there is a hope that seems to sustain or even propel the people forward. There are people who go out to work, college or classes every day. There is generally a hope that it will get better – the hope of getting their own place, having somewhere to bring their child on access visits, having a key to their own door. When this hope wanes it is the chaplain's role to help the person find it again, which isn't always easy. The care and generosity found among those who are homeless is beautiful to see; like carrying dinner for someone who is on crutches, the sharing of little treats that someone might have been given, sharing the last cigarette with someone who doesn't have one until payday, or the sharing of cigarette papers to make and share a smoke when someone has gone gathering butts to salvage a little tobacco to make a cigarette.

Community

Presence is a fundamental quality of chaplaincy. Joseph Jawarski described this as 'a profound opening of the heart, carried in to action'.[1] I experience this ongoing opening of heart in my ministry to men and women who experience homelessness as God's work in and through me. I was, and still am, transformed by those I meet as I move from a place of fear and lack of understanding to one of community and love. I hope that my presence among the people I walk with in homeless hostels reveals something of the unconditional, abundant love of God. At the Last Supper Jesus showed his apostles the type of ministry he desired – a humble service, illustrated by the washing of their feet. People who are homeless reveal many ways of being Christ to others and yes, even washing feet. Many have poured out the stories of their lives and have bathed my feet with acceptance, thereby helping me to walk barefoot through the hallowed places of their lives. They have revealed Christ to me.

1 P. Serge, C. O. Scharmer, J. Jawarski and B. S. Flowers, *Presence*, New York, NY: Double-day, 2005, 234.

10: The Military

Eoin Thynne

'Happy the peacemakers: they shall be called sons of God.'
Matthew 5:9

Reporting for Duty

As I reflect on a most rewarding and fulfilling ministry, I treasure many memories and value the lessons learnt. I can recall vividly the first day I 'reported for duty'. The young soldier who met me at the main gate of the barracks was polite, respectful and smartly turned out in uniform. I was looking forward to meeting and engaging with his colleagues. After the various introductions, I was taken on a tour of the barracks. To my surprise, instead of engaging with young, fighting-fit soldiers, I was introduced to two lads who would not have been out of place in *Dad's Army*! Not what I expected and not soldiers with whom I would choose to go to war! Friendly and welcoming, they were more than hospitable.

In the weeks that followed, the two 'old soldiers' appeared to spend their time loitering with intent, enjoying a smoke and passing the time in a more than relaxed manner. It was only some weeks later, when on exercise in the Glen of Imaal, that I fully appreciated the important role they played. While the action was happening on the battlefield, the non-glamorous tasks of setting up the tents and organising the rations were in the capable hands of the two most experienced soldiers in the battalion. Without their invaluable contribution and experience, the exercise could not have taken place and would not have been the success it was.

These two soldiers, who took me under their wing and marked my card on many occasions, demonstrated clearly that there is a role for everyone and each must play their part. We should appreciate those who do not conform to our expectations, but take the time to value their contribution and respect the uniqueness of every individual. Age should never be a barrier to what others can contribute.

It made me realise there are times when we have preconceived ideas or perhaps judge others by our own standards. There are those who do not always fit into the 'box' we have designed for them. We each have our own gifts and talents, perhaps not always obvious but always there.

Army Chaplains

Since the foundation of the Irish Volunteers in 1913, chaplains have been associated with Óglaigh na hÉireann (the Irish Army) but the first chaplains were not appointed to the Defence Forces until 1922. Chaplains work in all military environments with members of the Defence Forces, the Air Corps and the Naval Service. They hold a unique and valued position in that they are within the Defence Forces yet not of them; they are not strictly part of the chain of command, yet they uphold and respect the unique military command and control systems and work within them. As with chaplains in hospitals, schools, prisons etc. confidentiality is paramount; they respect the dignity and uniqueness of each person and are completely trustworthy.

One of the many advantages of army chaplaincy is the variety it offers. Patrolling our coastline in a gale force wind with Naval Service personnel demands courage, fearlessness and a good constitution. Could one ask for a more relaxing afternoon than observing the countryside from the 'eye in the sky' with those magnificent men in their flying machines from the Air Corps?

Understanding the System

I served as an army chaplain for twenty-five years, and it was a privilege to be afforded the opportunity to support the moral and spiritual well-being of military personnel and their families, whether they identified with a particular faith tradition, had no specific faith practice or were spiritually curious. A unique factor, and one that military personnel have in common, is that they tend to look upon things in the same way. They are recruited, educated and trained in the same tradition. The chaplain, however, looks upon things from another angle. Successful institutions and organisations realise that diversity is a strength and that it is important to exploit it. From my experience of service both at home and on overseas deployments, central to the specialised ministry of army chaplaincy is an understanding of the system within which the chaplains carry out their pastoral duties.

When I was first appointed chaplain, a senior officer explained how stressful and complicated joining a military organisation can be. 'It is not uncommon in the military world,' he said, 'for situations to arise quickly and solutions to be quickly found. There are many different expectations, not least of the chaplain. Always be and act as the person you are and use the skills that took you to this point in your ministry.' Standing up for one's Christian values and traditions or speaking on behalf of soldiers whose views and opinions are not always heard, may at times be in conflict with the system.

Whether at home or serving on an overseas' mission, it has been a privilege to reach out to men and women of different backgrounds, living with them and sharing their joys and sorrows. Sometimes, being available, just being there, is all that matters. Apart from administering the sacraments and officiating at liturgical celebrations and military ceremonies, much of my time was spent in the education and training, and the recreational and moral formation of recruits and cadets. There is a readiness among most military personnel to discuss and be responsive to religious issues and concerns.

Human Nature
Where human nature is at play, where there are rules and regulations, procedures and practices, it is inevitable there will be disputes and disagreements. In situations where 'conflict management' came into play, acting as an advocate for personnel of all ranks and offering a neutral and

Christian interpretation of events was very much part of my role.

I have learned from chaplaincy that nothing good comes by itself and nothing should be taken for granted. Army personnel are only too well aware that vehicles, weapons and all other pieces of equipment must be taken care of properly. The priority of a commander is to take care of his soldiers. If soldiers are 'broken', it doesn't matter how trimmed the vehicles are, how clean the weapons or how shiny the boots. The solider is always the most valuable asset and must be cared for in every aspect.

Tours of Duty

Overseas deployment holds many memories and is interwoven with moments of delight and occasions of tragedy. Military life requires a strict discipline, and discipline is possible only through self-sacrifice. Soldiers who serve overseas are ready even for the ultimate sacrifice, laying down their lives for their friends, the sacrifice that many of our soldiers have made. Irish soldiers have earned the blessing pronounced by Our Lord in the Gospel: 'Happy the peacemakers: they shall be called sons of God' (Matthew 5:9).

Lebanon provided many memories – tours of the Holy Land and the privilege of walking in the footsteps of Jesus. Sporting events against other contingents and the spirit of camaraderie and rivalry during inter-company competitions. For enthusiasm, celebration and excitement, the live televised Mass on RTÉ on Christmas Day 1993 is among the best of them. The sense of fun was captured in the logo displayed on our T-shirts, 'God, Me and RTÉ'!

The loss of life on tours of duty overseas will always remain etched on my mind. I can recall a particular tour of duty in the Lebanon, in the company of some of the toughest, most highly trained and fun-loving soldiers you are likely to find anywhere.

Having trained together as recruits, this band of brothers was as close as any tightly knit family. Their loyalty to one another was unquestionable, and it extended also to their superiors. Their resilience and courage was tested on the day one of the platoon was shot and fatally wounded. Prayers were offered, Mass celebrated and the incident and its effect on the troops were discussed with the personnel support service team.

As chaplain, I accompanied the cortège to the airport and offered the final prayers and blessing. The six soldiers who shouldered the coffin to the aircraft were paying their final respects to a brother, a buddy, a close friend. These young men, who were trained to endure hardship and operate in physically demanding situations, were true to their emotions as tears streamed down their cheeks. They were mourning the loss of a brother, now returning home to his original family. It is a moment that will always remain with me.

These young soldiers, lean, mean and equipped for war, were not ashamed to express their feelings and show their emotion. Military personnel, like so many of us, don't do the 'touchy-feely' stuff well, but the vulnerability we dared to touch brought out the human and gentle side of their character. There are times when we must all deal with our feelings and be true to ourselves.

Conclusion

As I reflect on my service as chaplain to the Defence Forces, the friendships that have endured, the lessons learned and the experience gained, I thank God for the opportunity to have been part of a specialised community whose core values of respect, loyalty, selflessness, physical courage, moral courage and integrity are the very fabric of its personnel. A very special ministry among very special people, and I am grateful to have been part of it. Buíochas mór le Dia.

11: The Secondary School

Gráinne Delaney

'Yours are the hands, yours are the feet,
yours are the eyes, you are his body.
Christ has no body now on earth but yours.'
Teresa of Ávila

The Role of a School Chaplain

When I began my job as school chaplain in Crescent College Comprehensive SJ in 1999, I was the first lay chaplain in the school's history. My predecessor left a list of retreat contacts on the desk, with his phone number. The principal gave me a list of ten things he would like to see happen in the school that year and told me to come back to him if I were too busy or too quiet! What is school chaplaincy about? The list from the principal included liturgies, retreats, fundraising, an idea about a bereavement programme and a direction to expand a section of the school library and encourage students to get to know their way around Jesuit books. I kept a keen eye on the list and ran school retreats for all classes, but it was quite some time before the pastoral care part of the role developed, as chaplaincy is all about relationships. And, indeed, those relationships have developed.

In a school setting a chaplain could spend a lot of time helping those who are having a bad day, or feeling overwhelmed. I see pastoral care as responding to the 'on the spot' upset for the students or meeting them on a one-to-one basis, listening and supporting while students are finding life hard. Pastoral care for me is a type of 'first aid', but it is important to separate it from counselling. Pastoral care can indeed lead to a referral for further expertise such as a counselling. I am always ready with the sticking plaster and the bandage, I even do regular and ongoing checkups, but for surgery and physiotherapy, there is further expertise available to schools. So it is important that chaplains are true to the spirituality of the role, along with the history and traditions of the institution. This has been the basis of the experience for me.

Ways of Being

Twenty-two years after my appointment as school chaplain, I reflect on the role and the work as it has evolved. I am confident that a spiritual, religious presence in the school, which holds hands with all that is good about well-being themes and teams, is still a very important component in Catholic education. Psychologist Shane Martin, in a recent presentation to teachers during Covid-19, spoke of his many years' experience working with people who were resilient, who had 'bounceability'. He spoke about six ways of being that keep people well, and one of the six was faith/prayer. Shane went on to clarify, 'I am not getting all holy now, I am just stating the fact that those who had prayer/faith as a regular part of their lives were more resilient and did better in terms of being able to cope and bounce back.'

In chaplaincy I have been offering students a journey of prayer and faith from First to Sixth Year, from the religion classroom, with animated conversations about sacraments, especially the most recent for them, confirmation, to academic learning about 'other religions'. The students display an appetite for it all. I often speak in the classroom about 'learning about a more grown-up version of God'. This timing is critical as confirmation for many twelve-year-olds is a graduation – out of the Church. It's over now. So, if their understanding of God was childlike, for example

> All knowing (like Santa)
> All powerful (looks unlikely)
> Decision-maker (like a judge)
> Controlling life (like a puppeteer)
> Handy when things go bad (call 999)

then I tempt them with something more grown up.

The Examen

Using the daily examen is one way to do this. It is a prayerful and beautiful way for them to look back over their day, to watch the video of their day in a spirit of gratitude. Gratitude helps people feel more positive emotions, relish good experiences, improve their health, deal with adversity and build strong relationships. Ultimately, they are asking the question, 'Can I talk to God about what has happened? Is my life different when I pray?' This is a really tempting invitation to students to pray in their own words and find God in all things (a characteristic of Jesuit education). This method and pattern of reflecting on experience is comforting when a girl arrives at my door in tears, saying, 'Something awful has happened, my day is ruined, everything is ruined. I need to go home.' I often watch the video of the student's day and examine what has happened for them during that day. Together we identify parts we need to deal with now and those they can put aside for later. We find ways to recover and live the rest of our day, here and now.

Experience

Frequently, the students call out to me when passing or chatting, 'Miss, when is our retreat?' I wonder what they are looking forward to really. A day off campus, a bus journey to somewhere they've never been before, a laugh, time with friends, time to get away from it all and reflect on how life is going, a conversation with and about God? These are the things students write about in their reflections after their retreats. Most important is the developmental nature of what they are offered from First to Sixth Year. The retreat experience grows and becomes more mature with the teenager. From learning meditation and dipping into pilgrimage with a riverbank walk in First Year, through a progression of action and reflection experiences, including social placement and life-graphing and affirmation exercises, to the ultimate overnight retreat in Sixth Year. These help students to pay attention to the part of the retreat that allows them to work on their 'relationship with self'. Sketching a graph that plots the positivity in their lives to date, and noting the challenges also, helps them to register that their life has patterns to which they should pay attention. When they affirm each other while on retreat by writing positive and encouraging messages in each other's journals, they are sending a message to their peers that they are 'worthwhile'. Peer affirmation is a very powerful tool in building self-confidence.

Other projects we take on are: a walking pilgrimage through the mountains; a self-awareness yoga retreat, an action/reflection retreat on the Dublin coast; and two days of quiet and prayer which they share with contemplative sisters in Waterford.

Leadership

What makes these experiences different from outdoor pursuits and team-building trips is the ongoing reflection which asks: Who am I? Who am I becoming? How is God leading me? They are indeed special spaces, and it is the chaplain's role to keep these questions to the fore in the education process. The chaplain must hand over the responsibility to be leaders in faith to the students, and they step up proudly. A female lay chaplain is an example to the students and staff of how normal life can be spiritual and spiritual life can be normal. I have enabled students to become ministers of the word, not merely reading reflections but leading prayer. It takes courage to stand before a full school assembly and say, 'Dear Lord'. It might be easier to read the sort of feel-good reflection more appropriately found on a greeting card. However, our senior students take such ownership of this that if you tried to take away the prayer at the start of school assembly, they would object. They see this as a strategy to hand on something tangible to the next generation. That is leadership. Our students train as eucharistic ministers and must write a letter of application about this faith step, which is not taken lightly. Students also step up as leaders in peer-led retreats and in morning prayer and learn skills they can take wherever they go in life.

Rhythm

In an increasingly secular world school chaplains are teaching school communities about the liturgical year, through visuals and the celebration of other special moments. A recent graduate said to my daughter, who is also a graduate, 'Am I living under a rock or did you know that yesterday was Ash Wednesday?' She added pensively, 'Of course if I were still in Crescent I would know. I distributed ashes at Mass there last year. This is the first year that the start of Lent has passed me by.' There are few liturgical reference points in society, so November remembrance, Advent wreaths, Lenten prayer and Easter celebrations are all bringing students through those special spiritual moments in the liturgical year that general society doesn't expose them to very much. In Crescent we are inviting students to walk to a rhythm that is different from the one found in the consumerist experience of life.

Conclusion

Chaplaincy matters, it is a privileged space, but I share a word of caution. While it is important to offer real and tangible programmes and experiences, the extreme manifestation of this is the chaplain who is too busy to provide pastoral support. With thirty-four buses going out the school gate this year, twenty-five students starting a leadership course next month, planning a graduation event for a thousand people, a desk covered with lists and budgets, how can a chaplain be 'available'? My wake-up call came when a boy stopped me to say, 'I was going to speak to you on Monday but you look so busy all the time'. The work of the school chaplain is to lead and facilitate opportunities for students to grow in relationship with self, others, God and Creation. It is also knowing, when a student comes to the door, to look calmly back at that student, put down the pen, close the laptop and be present to this privileged moment.

12: The Prison

Catherine Black

'For I know the plans I have for you, declares the Lord, plans to prosper you and not to harm you, plans to give you hope and a future.'
Jeremiah 29:11

Prison Ministry

I have had the privilege of serving as chaplain for the Irish Prison Service since 2016, First in Shelton Abbey open centre in Arklow, before moving to Mountjoy Male Prison, Dublin, in 2018. The two places are very different environments, but the ministry is the same: both are about being with men who are locked away, deprived of their liberty, men who are suddenly plucked from their normal lives, removed from their families, and are often labelled by society, men who are front page headlines for a day or two but are then swiftly hidden from society's gaze.

Mountjoy Prison has over 700 men behind high concrete walls on the outskirts of North Dublin. I am one among a team of chaplains. We have three full-time and two part-time chaplains working within the prison.

A Person First

Prison ministry is all about meeting the men *as they are now*; not reading newspaper stories that have made some of them infamous criminals. Of course, many of these men are dangerous and they need to be away from society, but they are also much more than that. They are the same as you or me: human beings made in the image and likeness of Jesus. This is uncomfortable for many of us to accept, but the heart of what we do as prison chaplains is to try to bring the possibility of redemption to every person we meet.

No matter what your background – privileged or impoverished, educated or not – once you find yourself in prison you are the same as every other prisoner. Once committed, each prisoner gets a number and is identified by that number until the end of their sentence. The prison system takes away your freedom to make choices for yourself. What time you get up at, when you take a shower, when you have lunch and dinner, when lights are turned on or off, all these things are controlled by the prison officers.

During the precious time out of their cells, prisoners can make a phone call to family members from a sometimes very noisy landing. This six-minute phone call is the only daily contact they will have with their families – the usual thirty-minute in-person visits once a week have been restricted to fifteen-minute online visits because of the Covid pandemic. Those prisoners who, for whatever reason, need to go on a protected regime, have only one hour outside their cells each day.

The Chaplain

I believe that everyone has the ability to change, to redeem themselves in the eyes of their family and society as a whole. How many of us can say that we've *never* done anything wrong? How many second chances have we had in our lives?

My role as chaplain is to advocate for the men in my care, to see their potential for change, to speak up for them at management meetings and with those who have authority over them. After all, we believe, as Christians, in the forgiveness offered freely by our ever-forgiving God in the Sacrament of Reconciliation. Likewise, the men who find themselves in prison deserve this forgiveness; it's their second chance to become positive members of their communities.

For many prisoners the chaplain is the only person who will ever see beyond their crimes. Many are truly sorry for and ashamed of the offences they've committed. They feel an unending guilt for the hurt they've inflicted – not only on their victims – but also on their own families and loved ones.

I've witnessed the suffering of children when they are separated from their fathers; it is painful to watch their confusion and sadness.

The World Outside

Meanwhile, life on the outside continues for the prisoners' families; birthdays, first communion, confirmation and births all go on without the prisoner being present. However, by far the hardest and most hurtful time for anyone in prison is when a loved one dies.

As chaplains, breaking bad news about the death of a mother, father, sister, brother or grandparent is one of the most important aspects of our pastoral care. This is a time when our ministry has the most profound impact on those we serve.

The small chaplaincy office located in the heart of the circle in Mountjoy has to be an oasis of calm and quiet – a stark contrast to the noise of heavy metal gates and shouting, which is the norm in the main body of the prison. Once a prisoner is invited into the chaplaincy office, he instinctively knows something is wrong. Quickly but calmly, I will tell him that his worst nightmare has come to pass: a special loved one has died. In the sanctuary and safety of the chaplaincy space, he will let the first waves of grief crash over him. When he have a moment of recovery, he is encouraged to phone his family to hear what happened at first hand.

At a time like this there is an urge to be with family, to be close to our nearest and dearest. For prisoners, however, this is not possible. They remain alone and separated, locked away from those closest to them. Chaplains try to provide that much-needed connectedness between prisoners and family at these darkest of times. Technology has helped enormously, of course, especially as Covid-19 now restricts all our movements; prisoners are able to view the funerals of their loved ones via webcam. I've found that watching and praying, along with the funeral liturgy, has a profound effect on the men. They can experience a change of heart and commit to turning their lives around. 'Life has changed, not ended' is an important and hopeful message at these times.

Inspiration

At this time of loss, and on many other occasions in the prison, I'm reminded that Jesus brings hope. Hope is indeed at the heart of what we try to do as we minister to the prisoners in our care. Hope and forgiveness are not always easy. The plight of prisoners sentenced to life imprisonment and some societal attitudes towards them present some of the biggest challenges. Often, I have to dig deep to find a way to forgive. However, I find inspiration when I contemplate the example Jesus gave to us on the cross. Having suffered excruciating pain at the hands of the soldiers, having been abused and betrayed by the crowd, and as the soldiers gambled for his clothes by throwing dice, he was able to say, 'Father, forgive them for they know not what they are doing!'

A Journey Towards Goodness

This level of forgiveness is beyond our human comprehension. How can we forgive someone who will put us to death? How can we forgive someone who has taken the life of a beloved family member? I don't know, and perhaps it is not possible to know. For the victim's family and close circle of friends, forgiving those who commit murder is hugely difficult if not impossible. As a prison chaplain I am very aware of the pain and hurt caused by the people I minister to. However, I also believe that not forgiving only hurts us more. Perhaps an answer lies somewhere within the mystery of the resurrection. If we truly believe that our loved one's life has not ended, but changed, and that we will all meet in life eternal, maybe as individuals and as communities we must find a place for even the most notorious of our prisoners. For many of the prisoners on a life sentence their own lives ended the moment they were responsible for the death of another. Most will say that they truly did not know what they were doing. Some of those killed were their closest friends. At that moment, life has changed, irreversibly, for everyone involved, and there is immense pain on all sides.

Conclusion

Just as Jesus preached a controversial message, I too am very conscious of my message of forgiveness for those who have caused us hurt and pain. My ministry demands that I leave room for the goodness of a person to emerge. I often witness their sense of pain and remorse, and I believe that everyone deserves a second chance. In Ireland, prisoners on a life sentence typically serve twenty years or more, and, depending on the circumstances, sometimes much more. Even on release they remain on licence, so the slightest breach of their parole conditions can result in their returning to prison. I've been involved in accompanying prisoners on days of resocialisation prior to their release. Most are carrying a heavy burden of guilt; this guilt never leaves them, yet they all want to prove to society, and to themselves and their families, that they have a positive contribution to make.

Chaplaincy within our prisons is certainly a ministry of hope. For the people I meet every day I must point to a future beyond the walls of Mountjoy. Hope is what keeps the men I meet alive, hope that one day they too will be allowed to reunite with their families and continue their long road to redemption.

13: The Healthcare Setting: The Hospice

Anna Kennedy

'I want to encourage you to lean into God's peace wherever you find it.
God is consistent and generous and abundant in guiding us
and in affirming his will with us.'
Enuma Okoro[1]

Quality of Life

Palliative care can instil fear when mentioned in any circumstance. When suggested in a medical setting, acute anxiety may ensue for the person living with a terminal illness and, also for any family member who may be present at the consultation. Sensitivity by all in the caring profession can ease the understandable anxiety for the person and for the family unit. As part of a supportive team, a chaplain can have considerable influence in lessening the distress.

Palliative care is holistic care, where the focus of care changes from treatments and therapies aimed at cure, to treatments and therapies aimed at comfort and support. According to the World Health Organization (WHO) the goal of palliative care must be 'the highest possible quality of life for both patient and family'. It is about caring for the whole person, acknowledging that one is a physical, psychological, social and spiritual being. Palliative care 'affirms life and regards death as a normal process'.[2]

Multi-disciplinary Team

No single discipline can know everything about a patient. However, in sharing their knowledge, members of the Multi-Disciplinary Team

---

1   Enuma Okoro, *Reluctant Pilgrim: A Moody, Somewhat Self-Indulgent Introvert's Search for Spiritual Community*, Nashville, TN: Fresh Air Books, 2010.
2   Department of Health and Children, *Report of the National Advisory Committee on Palliative Care*, Dublin, 2001, 20.

(MDT) can deliver a plan of care that is evaluated on an ongoing basis. The MDT consists of a member of staff from each discipline as well as a chaplain. The chaplain in this situation supports all patients, families, staff, volunteers and significant others, those who hold a religious belief and those whose belief does not have a religious content. The MDT also provides support for each team member through psychosocial meetings/ debriefing, as a way of reflecting on decisions taken and the challenges encountered in responding to the needs of patients and their families.

Within this team the chaplain represents God's loving, healing and accepting presence and 'seeks to convey God's care to those who suffer'.[3] Jesus considers the care given to another as given to himself (Matthew 25:40). This relationship highlights the fact that, as St Teresa of Avila wrote, 'Christ has no body on earth now but yours ...'. The Catholic chaplain, as a minister in this relationship, is 'responsible to God, to the one seeking pastoral service, to the ecclesial community,'[4] and to the hospice and health services.

Interrelated

A central principle of palliative care is a belief in the value of being present with a suffering person. Presence without addressing issues or voicing spiritual or religious ideas can be palliating and reassuring for the person. As Christians we believe all human beings are created in the image and likeness of God (Genesis 1:27), which invokes a deep respect for the sacredness of the other. Furthermore, we are interrelated beings, with God, with one another, with self and with creation. Within this context the Catholic chaplain is committed to pastoral presence, which strives to liberate and heal her suffering brothers and sisters. 'Pastoral care is holistic, though its primary concern is the spiritual dimension. [...] The pastoral care-giver's skills enable a person to own and utilise their strengths and those of the Church to facilitate healing.'[5]

3   John Quinlan, *Pastoral Relatedness – The Essence of Pastoral Care*, Lanham, MD: University Press of America, 2002, 7.
4   Richard M. Gula SS, *Ethics In Pastoral Ministry*, Mahwah, NJ: Paulist Press, 20.
5   J. Quinlan, op. cit., 24.

In this relationship a chaplain recognises the value of the guidance of the Holy Spirit.

Caring for People

To demonstrate the chaplain's role within holistic palliative care, I will share some experiences that stand out for me. For reasons of confidentiality I have changed all names. One encounter that stands out for me is a visit to Katie. An urgent phone call from our Community Palliative Care (CPC) nurse, Majella, required an immediate response, as tomorrow might be too late.

Katie's daughter Mary greeted me at the door. Mary, in praise of her mum's faith, shared how her attendance at Mass and prayer sustained her. She also shared about how much Katie looked forward to her grandchildren's visits when she was able for them. Katie looked very cosy in her bed; her acknowledgement of my presence when I greeted her was minimal. We continued to include her in our conversation and asked if she, or other family members, would wish to join in prayer. On Mary's invitation the room was soon filled with many people, including grandchildren and great-grandchildren – they wanted to be with her in a meaningful way. As they assembled, I noted the images and pictures in the room which gave me a clue as to how we might pray. In their sharing of stories the children also suggested some of Katie's favourite prayers. This set the scene for the prayers for a person as death approaches.

Another significant encounter happened on Christmas morning in the hospice. Mark, a very distressed man, lay in his bed with his head slightly over the side. On first greeting, he did not respond and, unsure if he was awake, I sat quietly for a moment, then, touching his hand gently, I said, 'Sr Anna, chaplain here.' With that Mark raised his head onto the pillow and lay quietly. I asked him how he was feeling. He suddenly sat up in the bed: 'You're asking me how I am feeling? I am [expletive] … dying.' Then, pointing towards a patient in the next bed, he said, 'He is [expletive] … dying too, and you are asking me how I am feeling?' A brief pause before Mark declared, 'Life is a waste.' When I asked him if his life was a waste, he responded, 'No.' 'What was good about it?' I asked. To this Mark replied, 'My children.' He spoke about them for a short time, then lay back on the pillow and went to sleep. This seemed to be enough to bring him peace, as he spoke little after that, and died within two days.

Alan, a young married man with children, who continued working and supporting his family in spite of being very ill, requested a chaplain's visit. When I visited him in his comfortable home, he shared how family life was good for him. He loved his children and had hoped that he would have a few years to 'get them on their feet'. He chatted about his Catholic childhood but said that he had lapsed. 'I have no reason for this, just stopped,' he said. Our conversation continued and then I asked him, 'As chaplain, is there anything I could do for you today?' His response came as a surprise. 'My greatest desire is to believe in God again, before I die.' He repeated it with a sense of urgency. I needed a moment of quiet to ask the Holy Spirit to guide me, then I said, 'Alan, the desire is enough for now.' 'Do you mean that?' he asked. I again repeated that 'the desire is enough for now'. It was as if the sun shone on his face. I said quietly, 'Thank you, God!' Alan died three days later.

On visiting Eileen's family following her death, her son Joe, who had arrived from Australia, welcomed me and we joined other family members. Mary, Eileen's daughter and main carer, talked about the difficulty they were experiencing in coming to an agreement on the funeral arrangements. Each wished to celebrate their Mum's life, but in different ways. Mary encouraged me to stay. I remained as a listening presence, after which we gathered around Eileen's bed for a prayer. Perhaps my presence as chaplain, accompanying Eileen's family, made a difference. Mary relayed this to the CPC nurse Paul the following day.

Conclusion

As a Catholic chaplain ministering within the ethos of the palliative care model, my understanding of the concept of caring and of the theology of ministry as expressed in the Catholic tradition has deepened. I believe that an attentive listening presence facilitates the development of a close empathetic relationship with patient, family and others. Within this relationship I offer a ministry that is rooted in my faith, remembering that each patient is a person with a spirituality and may wish to express it with a companion, someone just 'being there'. In time this may facilitate an unfolding of a belief system, which helps the patient find peace and retain hope throughout the stages of illness and dying. Some patients had no inclination or desire to receive the sacraments or participate in ritual or prayer, yet they found comfort, solace and peace. Others over time moved from a place of expressed 'no need' to a sacred space in which they were able to connect with their spiritual selves. Yet again, some specifically requested prayer, ritual and/or sacraments, a healing movement that is holistic.

Somehow, in the remembering and the telling of one's life story, God's gentle presence can break through to rediscover the treasures that endure and bring refreshing peace.

> So long Thy power hath blest me, sure it still
> Will lead me on.
> O'er moor and fen, o'er crag and torrent, till
> The night is gone,
> And with the morn those angel faces smile,
> Which I have loved long since, and lost awhile.
>
> (John Henry Newman, 'Lead Kindly Light')

14: The Migrant

John McCarthy

'A parish without boundaries is at the heart of migrant chaplaincy.
The unconditional love of God is the catalyst for
what we do and why we do it.'
John McCarthy

Serving the Whole Person

There are many aspects to migrant chaplaincy, and all are rooted in the Gospel message of God's unconditional love of everyone. Most of my ministry to migrants has been one of service to our Irish migrants to the United States at the Irish Pastoral Centre (IPC) in Boston. They often find themselves in dire straits with no one to lean on for help and support. Chaplaincy consists of many programme elements that meet the needs of the whole person, physically, spiritually and emotionally. Some argue that migrant chaplaincy is the provision of sacramental services alone. However, it is my belief that we cannot set about providing sacramental needs while ignoring the needs of the whole human person.

One need go no further than the Gospel to find inspiration for the role of chaplain. It is my hope that what I say can be applied to our experience in Ireland today as we welcome new communities to our land and provide chaplains to walk alongside them.

Cultural Competency

The concept of chaplaincy is rooted in Christian values of service to others, especially those in greatest need. In recent years, there has been a greater understanding of cultural competency when providing services. With cultural competency comes a deep understanding on the part of the chaplain of where the person is coming from, their openness to services, and the cultural biases related to their receiving of services. For the programmes to work, the chaplain must be able to show understanding and compassion, and to exercise non-judgemental listening and questioning. All these factors must be present if you are to develop a relationship of trust with the person or group you are working with. Cultural competency was key to the success of my ministry in Boston. I worked with a great team at the IPC where we offered a wide range of programmes including senior programmes; mother/toddler support group; immigration services; employment resources; and summer student support. In addition to these services we offered a comprehensive chaplaincy outreach programme. This pastoral ministry programme provided outreach and support to immigrants who were home-bound, incarcerated, grieving or in need of referrals for counselling. It supported and advocated for the rights of long-term prisoners and short-term detainees awaiting trial and deportation primarily due to circumstances surrounding their undocumented status. Prisoners and detainees were at high risk for depression and suicide, and clients received personal visits, legal assistance and compassionate counselling, as well as referrals to appropriate professional support through our strong Catholic networks.

Sacraments and Transitions

Celebrating the sacraments with the Irish community offered a unique opportunity to rekindle the faith of lapsed Catholics and remind them of the power of God's love regardless of past and current circumstances. They often felt estranged in their new setting and missed the intimacy of the liturgical practices of their homeland. Immigrants wanted to have their children baptised, so this was a great way to connect with families and develop long-lasting relationships of trust and mutual respect. Weddings were an excellent opportunity to further connect with the community and extend the outreach within the larger immigrant community.

While accepting that death is a natural progression to eternal life, we still must deal with the loss and the grief we experience when faced with death. Sudden accidental deaths and deaths by suicide leave those left behind struggling to cope with the trauma. The chaplain was always a welcome guest in people's homes after the death of a loved one. Family members welcomed the emotional support while planning the services. It is not easy sitting for hours with the young friends and family members of a suicide victim who are struggling to understand why they missed the signs. They are often tortured by guilt and grief. It is during these challenging times that people are open to prayer and a reminder that death is a natural progression to eternal life. An important part of my work was to do follow-up visits to further develop the relationships and remind people of the unconditional love of God. The key to a successful chaplaincy is to use all encounters with immigrants, no matter how sad, to promote the importance of Church, faith and God's love, which is at the heart of the Gospel and people's lives.

Prison and Detention

Prison ministry was one of the most rewarding parts of my chaplaincy work. Most of the long-term prisoners had been abandoned by their families and friends in the United States. Forgiveness was not something that the prisoners felt they deserved. Family members in Ireland had no means of communicating with the incarcerated and this left the prisoners feeling abandoned and often left to die in prison. I worked very closely with the Irish Chaplaincy for Prisoners Overseas (ICPO), based in Maynooth, who were a huge support to the prisoners and also to me as chaplain. With the ICPO and the assistance of the Irish Consulate in Boston, I was able to develop meaningful connections with family members back in Ireland and provide updates on a regular basis.

In addition, I worked with short-term detainees who were incarcerated due to their undocumented status. Immigrants went from living normal lives with spouses and children to being locked up waiting for a court hearing and ultimate deportation. The most difficult part was the waiting, waiting for a court hearing to answer to a misdemeanour, waiting for sentencing and waiting for deportation. Regular visitations were important due to the high risk of depression and anxiety. The prison system would break the strongest among us, so the presence of a chaplain who could bring a message of hope sustained many through to deportation.

Resurrection

Chaplaincy outside the context of Christianity is a series of support systems intended to bring comfort and relief to the afflicted. These services may lead to relief from suffering and pain and a better quality of life. Such services are readily available to the immigrant community and are provided by various non-profits and other community groups that are not affiliated with the Church. Services are conditionally based on need and income level. Their efficacy is contingent upon the willingness of the recipient to participate actively in the recovery process or take the steps necessary to make changes. Chaplaincy, while working alongside many of these services, has a remarkably different character and ethos. Often, making lifestyle changes without consideration of a 'higher power' has been proven to be unsustainable. Historically, the Catholic Church has viewed chaplaincy as the ultimate response to the resurrection. It embodies the idea that God's love is unconditional and that we can make a paradigm shift and view our lives through a new lens, the lens of the resurrection, a resurrection that opened new opportunities for us, the possibility of a completely new life with endless possibilities.

Conclusion

Chaplaincy has been a blessing in my life. Being able to minister to the immigrant community in Boston has had a profound impact on my faith life. It has deepened my faith and enriched my vocation in a way I never imagined. I went to give and I ended up receiving more than I could ever have anticipated. I feel more comfortable with the God who journeys alongside us than the God who appears trapped in our institutions and from which many feel alienated. As Pope Francis said, 'Displaced people offer us this opportunity to meet the Lord, even though our eyes find it hard to recognise him: his clothing in tatters, his feet dirty, his face disfigured, his body wounded, his tongue unable to speak our language.' The humbling experience of driving eight hours to visit an immigrant incarcerated for murder has taught me the power of compassion and forgiveness. When you walk in someone else's shoes you are walking in God's shoes. When you do for the prisoner what you would do for your own family, you are doing God's work. You bring hope to the hopeless, love to the unloved and peace to the troubled soul. I have met the Lord through my chaplaincy.

15: The Healthcare Setting: The Psychiatric Hospital

Hugh Gillan

The way we listen to God the Father is how we should listen to his faithful people. If we do not listen in the same way, with the same heart, then something has gone wrong.

Pope Francis[1]

An Amazing Journey

Over the past fifty years, a quiet revolution has taken place in the area of healthcare chaplaincy. This has been very evident within the Catholic Church. We have come from a time when the role was confined to priests, to a time when any suitably qualified person can apply to be a healthcare chaplain.

For the past twenty years I have worked as a chaplain in St John of God Psychiatric Hospital, and it has been an amazing journey for me. As a brother of St John of God, living a life dedicated to serving the sick, the poor and the needy, following the Lord by trying to walk in the footsteps of our founder has been a great challenge, but a very worthwhile one.

To fulfil my role I am very much aware that, as a chaplain in a hospital setting, I am unable to meet every patient individually. However, there is a need to have a sense of connectedness with as many patients as possible. In order to achieve this I usually visit every ward in the hospital twice a day. This gives me the opportunity to meet with staff who can inform me if there is someone who may benefit from a visit by me. It allows me to introduce myself to patients I haven't met before. I also meet patients in the coffee shop or out in the grounds. Greeting them by name is very important to them.

1 Pope Francis, *With the Smell of the Sheep: the Pope Speaks to Priests, Bishops, and Other Shepherds*, Maryknoll, NY: Orbis Books, 2017.

Spirituality and Mental Health

For very many people, their spirituality is often expressed and experienced through religious beliefs. It is acknowledged in the field of psychiatry that spirituality can play a very important role in helping people maintain good mental health and can also help them on their journey to recovery from mental health issues.

A person admitted to a psychiatric hospital is usually struggling with mental health issues, addictions and eating disorders that cause pain, hurt, distress and much suffering. As a result, they become disconnected from their relationships and they need support to reconnect with themselves, with others, with God/higher power and with their environment. This, I believe, is the function of the multi-disciplinary team as a whole, in which the chaplain plays an integral and specific role, as spiritual companion to each patient – helping, assisting and guiding patients in their concerns with the ultimate questions about life's meaning, which may or may not arise from formal religious traditions.

Three Responses

Some months ago I was reading a book by Pope Francis called *With the Smell of the Sheep*.[2] One of the articles spoke very powerfully to me and, as a chaplain, it was a message I needed to hear and heed. Pope Francis speaks about the Gospel story of Bartimaeus, the 'blind beggar', and how the followers of Jesus reacted when they encountered this man. The Pope says, 'There were three responses to the cry of the blind man and today these three responses are also relevant. We can describe them with three phrases taken from the Gospel: "Pass by", "Be quiet", "Take heart and get up".'

He continues: 'Some of Jesus' followers did not even hear the shouts of Bartimaeus and they passed him by. However, they wanted to hear what Jesus had to say.' Commenting on their command for Bartimaeus to 'Be quiet!', Pope Francis writes:

2   Ibid.

This is the second response to Bartimaeus's cry: 'Keep quiet, don't bother us, leave us alone' … this is the attitude of some of the leaders of God's people. They continually scold others. Please embrace them, listen to them, and tell them that Jesus loves them.

The crowd's third response, 'Take heart and get up', is a reaction of the people who saw how Jesus responded to the pleading of the blind beggar. When they see Jesus' reaction they change their attitudes. Jesus stops and asks the man, 'What do you want me to do for you?' Pope Francis continues, 'He simply asked him a question, looked at him, and sought to come into his life, to share his lot. And by doing this he gradually restored the man's lost dignity.' For me, in this address, I feel that Pope Francis is asking me to come out of my 'comfort zone' and reflect on how to be a good chaplain.

The chaplain provides spiritual input in the occupational therapy and addiction programmes in the hospital. In addition to spiritual care, religious services also have an important part to play in ministering to people in the hospital community. All patients have the right to have access to a minister from their own faith community. The hospital also respects the patients' right to choose not to participate in religious activities, as well as the right to request no spiritual input in their care plan. The hospital has a chapel as well as a multi-faith prayer room, allowing for a diversity of religious practices amongst patients, within a culture of hospitality. The celebration of the Eucharist takes place every day except Friday and there is a healing service once a month. The Sacrament of Reconciliation and the Sacrament of the Sick are available on request.

I am amazed when patients stop me and ask for a blessing. Some of the reasons they give are, 'I'm feeling a bit down today', 'I don't think I'm getting better', or 'I want God to help me get better soon'. While such requests are occasional, they highlight how, in the depths of their distress and struggles, some patients come to recognise their need for a merciful God to assist them and be with them

Spiritual Strength and Faith Inspiration

As working with patients who have mental health issues can be quite challenging, I need to be aware of my own inner resources and frequently reflect on what gives me the strength to do my work. One of the sources from which I draw much strength is the story of the life of St John of God (1495–1550), a man who dedicated the last eleven years of his life to serving the poor, the sick and the needy in the city of Granada, Spain. Before beginning his ministry to the sick, John owned and worked in a small bookshop. We are told that after listening one day to a sermon given by John of Ávila, the bookseller, who was a religious man, reacted 'very strangely'. He went to his bookshop, tore up all the non-religious books and then went out into the streets proclaiming himself to be a 'great sinner'. Two gentlemen who knew him took him to the Royal Hospital for the 'insane' where he remained for several months. Having made a good recovery, he reflected on his time in the hospital and the cruel treatment he and the other patients received. He had prayed to God to give him the opportunity, when he left the hospital, to establish his own hospital where he could treat people with all the dignity and respect that they deserved. Within a short period of time that is exactly what he did. And the rest, as they say, is history!

I receive a lot of encouragement and hope by responding daily to my vocation as a St John of God brother/priest. Consecrated life gives me so many opportunities to pay close attention to the spiritual dimension of my life on a daily basis. Daily Eucharist, community and private prayer greatly help me in my personal life but also give me strength in my ministry as a chaplain. The old saying 'you cannot give what you haven't got', makes a lot of sense to me.

Conclusion

I have written mainly about caring for patients in the hospital, but there is also an amount of work done in reaching out to the members of staff and occasionally to family members. It is so inspiring to see a person with mental health issues begin their journey of recovery in the hospital and succeed in getting back to good health again. To realise that many have endured psychological and spiritual struggle, pain and hurt in their lives, and that as a healthcare chaplain you have journeyed with them, helping them to be well again, can be a humbling but also an enriching experience. A deep and satisfying realisation comes over me when I recall the words of Jesus in the Gospel of Matthew, 'As long as you did it to one of these sisters and brothers of mine, you did it to me' (Matthew 25:40).

16: The University

Sarah O'Rourke and John Campion

'I remind you to keep alive the gift that God gave you ... for the Spirit that God has given us does not make us timid; instead, his Spirit fills us with power, love and self-control.'
2 Timothy 1:6–7

God's Dream

As chaplains at the University of Limerick (UL), we are an integral part of the Student Affairs Division of the university. We are members of the Salesian congregation who are inspired by the vision of Don Bosco and Mary Mazzarello, whose legacy tells us they were weavers of relationships, believers in the inherent goodness and divine destiny of every person, prophets of compassion and ministers of hope and joy. As educators they listened empathetically to those they encountered. They took an interest in the circumstances of their lives, thus allowing people, especially the young, to find their innate potential. For Don Bosco, 'Relationship is at the heart of education', and Mary Mazzarello advised, 'It is necessary to study the individual character and to know each one so as to succeed well and inspire confidence'.

The poem 'God's Dream', by French poet Charles Péguy (1873–1914), makes a lot of sense when we pause to reflect on chaplaincy at third level:

I myself will dream a dream within you ...
It is my dream you dream
my house you build
my caring you witness
my love you share,
and this is the heart of the matter.

As chaplains it is this dream of God that 'is the heart of the matter'. This leads us to wonder in what ways we can live out this dream of God on a university campus with over 16,300 students and 1,700 staff.

Chaplaincy and the University

In his words of welcome to the 2014 Annual CN3 Conference hosted by UL Chaplaincy, the then president, Don Barry, captured the contribution that chaplains make to the university community:

> Every chaplain already knows this, but it bears saying again, with the greatest of respect and appreciation – chaplains add immense value and comfort to the lives of a university community. They provide a vital service and a listening ear to our students and staff and strive to meet the changing needs of our global university community. Teach Fáilte, our Chaplaincy Centre, is a popular drop-in centre where visitors join together and examine faith and belief, share religious texts and communicate and celebrate through music and culture. Our Contemplative Centre offers a quiet oasis for prayer and personal reflection. These spaces are intentionally designed to bring people closer together and I know that our chaplains perform a critical, often unseen and unheralded role to bridge gaps, heal differences and forge and nourish relationships that are vital to our sense of community and the welfare of our campus community.

Strategic to the operation of UL Chaplaincy are the intentionally designed Teach Fáilte and Contemplative Centre on the campus. They afford the chaplains space to offer opportunities for worship, and to provide welcome, pastoral care and support to facilitate spiritual engagement and reflection and to encourage social responsibility and volunteerism.

A Place of Welcome

Teach Fáilte, located in the Student Square, is the face and the hub of the chaplaincy services. The presence of a chaplain in Teach Fáilte is key to the implementation of our mission statement of being 'a holistic, inclusive service aimed at the authentic development of the human person for students and staff of all faiths and none'. Chaplaincy provides a listening service that responds and reacts to the ebb and flow of life whether that is tragedy and loss or joy and achievement.

Teach Fáilte attracts over 500 students weekly. This high number is due to the eclectic services found there, which include: a safe home-away-from-home atmosphere and facilities for UL students and staff; space for students to chat, get to know each other and exchange stories of the ordinary and not so ordinary; and support for students who need encouragement as they navigate their way through the academic cycle. The chaplaincy also supports activities and events such as the UL President's Volunteering Award, which includes the opportunity of volunteering in liturgical ministry, social media administration and as 'meet and greet' hosts. As part of this award all volunteers complete a reflective portfolio.

A Place of Support

Teach Fáilte's greatest value lies in the pastoral care and counselling bridge it offers to vulnerable students who may not seek help elsewhere. The chaplains are very aware that the presenting issue is not always the key one for which the student needs support. These include students coping with bereavement, loneliness, family concerns, relationship break-up, addiction, sexual orientation, chronic illness, financial difficulties, seeking asylum and a more general search for meaning. In times of difficulty students are assured of a non-judgemental listening ear and may be facilitated to avail of other supports on or off campus. During the Covid-19 pandemic, chaplains were unable to provide the hospitality of the boiling kettle, but they continued to remotely provide the hospitality of listening. Some students found it difficult to adjust to online learning and others felt socially isolated. Many missed face-to-face contact but appreciated the 'space to be listened to' over the phone. From experience we know the wisdom of the Irish proverb, 'Giorraíonn beirt bóthar' – two people shorten the road.

A Place of Peace

Staff and students are encouraged to avail of the Contemplative Centre, which is an oasis of peace and tranquillity. This is a sacred space for quiet, meditation, prayer, reflection and sacramental moments. It is here that people take time to open the word of God and break bread. Throughout the academic year, bespoke inter-faith and denominational services are held for special occasions of celebration or tragedy. It has been a longstanding UL tradition to host an annual remembrance service. During the Covid-19 pandemic, support to the bereaved from the wider UL community was not available as before. The chaplains, with the assistance of the President's Office, the Irish World Academy of Music and Dance and volunteer students, offered a virtual service. This provided a measure of consolation to those who are grieving and was an opportunity to collectively reflect and take time to remember. The Contemplative Centre is also available for group gatherings and visiting speakers. The chaplaincy provides an inter-faith directory where staff and students can meet people of varied faith traditions in UL and in the Mid-West region. Inter-faith calendars are on display in the Contemplative Centre as well as in Teach Fáilte. At present there are ongoing negotiations for a memorial garden as well as a larger prayer space for the Muslim community. All of our faiths can share and come together in the dream of God.

Conclusion

We continue to share a journey with those we encounter, and we walk with hope-filled hearts, ever mindful that we are sharers of a dream entrusted to us:

I myself will dream a dream within you …
Good dreams come from me, you know.
My dreams seem impossible,
not too practical,
not for the cautious man or woman
a little risky sometimes
a trifle brash perhaps.
Some of my friends prefer
to rest comfortably,
in sounder sleep,
with visionless eyes.
But, from those who share my dreams
I ask a little patience
a little humour,
some small courage,
and a listening heart.
I will do the rest.
Then they will risk
and wonder at their daring.
Run … and marvel at their speed ….
Build … and stand in awe at the beauty of their building.
You will meet me often as you work
in your companions, who share the risk
in your friends, who believe in you enough
to lend their own dreams
their own hands
their own hearts
to your building.
In the people who will stand in your doorway,
stay a while,
and walk away knowing that they, too, can find a dream.
There will be sun-filled days,

and sometimes it will rain
a little variety –
both come from me.
So come now, be content.
It is my dream you dream
my house you build
my caring you witness
my love you share,
and this is the heart of the matter.

Sarah O'Rourke and John Campion

17: The Seafarer

Siobhán O'Keeffe

'May the Lord bless each of you, your work and your families,
and may the Virgin Mary, Star of the Sea, protect you always.'
Pope Francis

Volunteering

My love of the sea was born unexpectedly one Saturday morning in April 1979 when our Leaving Certificate geography teacher took us on a trip around Cork harbour. The following year I embarked on my nurse training in Liverpool and returned home regularly on the overnight Liverpool–Dublin ferry. My song of praise rang deep in my soul as we docked in Irish waters (Psalm 40:3). On completion of my training I left Liverpool and returned in 1987 when, after suffering a deep personal disappointment, a good friend encouraged me to volunteer one evening a week at the Apostleship of the Sea, an agency of the Catholic Church founded in Glasgow in the early twentieth century to provide pastoral care to seafarers through chaplaincies in ports in all continents of the world. I was deeply moved by the courage and generosity of this global community, who sacrifice many years of shared family life in their silent ethic of service to us all. Most of our communication was non-verbal, but a smile or an act of kindness crosses all oceans. My life, spirit and faith were deeply enriched by this encounter.

Who are Seafarers?

Seafarers come from many countries, with the highest proportion from China, the Philippines, Indonesia, the Russian Federation and India. Women make up just 2 per cent of the workforce. Many sailors leave their homes for many months at a time to navigate the oceans to complete their mission of delivering 90 per cent of the world's trade for industry, healthcare and homemaking. The recent Suez Canal crisis when the *Ever Given* container ship was grounded, blocking the free flow of 10–12 per cent of goods across the world, highlighted the vulnerability of the shipping industry and its impact on the lives of many. This is a visible example of the vulnerability of life on the seas which results in much suffering for seafarers and their families.

A Way of Life

Many seafarers come from poor countries with limited employment opportunities. There seafaring is a way of life for entire families going back generations. As in biblical times, life on the seas can be very harsh as seafarers are at risk from cruel seas (Mark 4:37). In some circumstances they are exploited, do not receive good quality food, rest breaks or adequate medical cover. The constant drone of the engine or unhealthy fumes can have a negative impact on the physical and mental well-being of the person. Wages may be withheld, or terms of employment changed without notice. The suffering of seafarers was aggravated by the Covid-19 pandemic when they were unable to return home, an issue highlighted by Pope Francis in a message to seafarers when he said, 'Long periods spent aboard ships without being able to disembark, separation from families, friends and native countries, and fear of infection, are a heavy burden to bear.' Highlighting the importance of the work of port chaplains, he went on to say,

> Today I would like to offer you a message and a prayer of hope, comfort and consolation in the face of whatever hardships you have to endure … I would also offer a word of encouragement to all those who work with you in providing pastoral care for maritime personnel.

Pastoral Care

Inspired by the pastoral response of Pope Francis, I believe that chaplaincy can offer much comfort and hope to all who suffer. This is fleshed out in the ministry of the Apostleship of the Sea, whose mission is 'to welcome all seafarers in the name of Christ when they arrive in port and to minister to their pastoral, spiritual and welfare needs'. To do this effectively, I believe that chaplains and chaplains' assistants should be appointed to the whole maritime community to care pastorally for both crew and management. Decisions about the pastoral needs of each group should be made in consultation with them so that the service provided responds to their needs. When organising a chaplaincy service for ports, 'the ethnic and cultural mix of the ships' community and even more specifically, the religious affiliation of those who will avail of the service should be taken into consideration. It must be borne in mind that ethnicity is no indicator of religion' (my adaptation from the *Handbook on Hospital Chaplaincy* to reflect the needs of the seafaring community).

The Role of a Port Chaplain

A chaplain can offer a level of pastoral care that is much broader than that traditionally associated with pastoral theology. It is something that permeates and enriches the entire community. The chaplain has an important role and responsibility to ensure that justice for all is upheld, and may act as a voice for those who face injustices by challenging unjust working structures, poor resources, discrimination, exploitation and any form of abuse (see Proverbs 31:8).

For those for whom sacraments and ritual are important the role of chaplains cannot be underestimated, but their contribution is not only to those for whom religious ritual is important. A chaplain is a pastoral person whose primary concern is 'being with' the person who needs ministry. This concern is manifest in the following ways: attending to the religious and spiritual needs of staff, shipping companies and port authorities in prayer or ritual; providing general support to staff; acting as an advocate or mediator between staff and management in difficult situations; providing general emotional support for individual staff; providing education and training to staff groups to heighten awareness; acting as an advocate or mediator between groups of staff; giving advice to the shipping company on ethical issues and consulting with the shipping or port authority on general policy issues. The pastoral care offered by a port or maritime chaplaincy service calls for collaboration of statutory and Church bodies so that the highest quality of care can be offered to the maritime community and their families.

When bad news is received, grief is compounded by the person's inability to be with their family or loved ones at a time of great suffering. The compassionate presence and embrace of the chaplain can help the grieving person to 'deal with ultimate issues and concerns'[1] and so help the person to deal more fully with their difficulties.

Joys and Hopes

As a Christian, and a sister of the Sacred Hearts of Jesus and Mary, I believe that the pastoral dimension of care offered by a chaplaincy service can help the shipping authorities to listen to the expressed felt needs of all staff and their families. What do staff say that they need? As disciples of Jesus we are called to listen to and respond to 'the joys and hopes, the griefs and anxieties of the people of this age, especially those who are poor or in any way afflicted'.[2] We are called to bear witness to the Gospel, serve the people of God and share in the transformative mission of Jesus in the world. In this context the maritime world will come to know more fully a gospel message of liberation.'[3] The chaplaincy service will bear witness to its mission to help people know and uphold their dignity, which 'is rooted and perfected in God'[4] and so 'share in the happiness

1   W. Clebsch and C. Jaekle, *Pastoral Care in Historical Perspective*, New York, NY: Harper, 1967.
2   Second Vatican Council, *Gaudium et Spes, Pastoral Constitution On the Church in the Modern World*, 1965, 7.
3   D. Bosch, *Transforming Mission*, Maryknoll, NY: Orbis Books, 2000, 177.
4   *Gaudium et Spes*, 21:2.

of God'.[5] It is against this backdrop that the importance of incorporating Gospel values and positive pastoral care as expressed through chaplaincy into the economic world is essential. When this takes place all who sail on the seas and dock in the ports of the world will share in the fullness of life that Christ wishes to offer to all people. 'I have come that you may have life and have it to the full' (John 10:10).

5   Ibid.

18: The Healthcare Setting: The Hospital

John Kelly

'The specialist and unique role of healthcare chaplains displays Christ's interest in persons in their various aspects: physical, social, emotional and spiritual. Each person is at the centre of what a Healthcare Chaplain does and the essential role of healthcare chaplaincy is to keep the complete person in view.'
Neville A. Kirkwood[1]

The Setting

In my role as a healthcare chaplain, I constantly remind myself that on the road to Emmaus (Luke 24:13–35) Jesus becomes a companion to the two disciples; he simply falls into step with the two figures as they walk: two people who are dejected, devastated, confused, nothing making sense, searching for answers. Jesus listens as they both articulate the experiences they have been through and express how they feel about themselves. Through his active and attentive listening, Jesus gives them hope and a new perspective to sustain them.

In the university hospital where I work, over 3,000 staff of fifty-seven different nationalities care for over 16,000 inpatient admissions per year as well as 227,000 outpatient visits and 49,000 emergency department attendances. There are over 550 deaths in the hospital each year. I am a member of a pastoral care team comprising nine chaplains from the four main Christian faiths, and sixty volunteer ministers of the Eucharist. The service is provided by ordained and non-ordained chaplains and is offered irrespective of faith tradition, life philosophy or personal world-view.

---

1   Neville A. Kirkwood, *Pastoral Care in Hospitals*, Harrisburg, PA: Church Publishing, Inc., 2005.

A Place of Vulnerability

In my role I find myself working in the dark places of sickness, fear and death with patients and their families. The relationship of being present to and caring for staff twenty-four hours a day is of critical importance to my supportive role and is a unique contribution of chaplaincy. Working alongside colleagues in the clinical environment provides them with on-the-spot support when dealing with distressing events or complex cases.

The work of healthcare chaplains is carried out not in the certainty of faith and religion but in the complex world of insecurity, vulnerability and fear. The pastoral relationship is uniquely non-medical and is focused on the person rather than the illness. It is an intrinsic part of the delivery of person-centred care. Healthcare chaplains work with colleagues to provide the best possible support to patients during some of the most difficult experiences any of them will ever have to face. The chaplains are embodied reminders of the way in which spirituality and religion are connected to the ancient and sacred tasks of healing and caring for sick persons.[2] This specialist role shows its likeness to Christ's ministry by sensitively and compassionately meeting a person at his or her point of need: physical, social, emotional and spiritual.[3]

Conveyer of Life

A hospital bed presents a person with time to think and to reflect on a changed perspective on life. In an instant, a happy and fulfilled life can be brought to a standstill through sickness. Patients question themselves, their past, their present and what the future may hold for them. I listen daily to patients pouring out their hearts and grappling with the deep questions that matter most to them: Why is this happening to me? What have I done wrong? Will I die? I hold these conversations, these sacred places – not filling them with words – as I actively listen

---

2 Bruce Rumbold et al., 'Models of spiritual care 177', in *Oxford Textbook of Spirituality in Healthcare*, Oxford: Oxford University Press, 2012, 175.
3 Neville A. Kirkwood, op. cit.

and respond to the things of the human spirit.[4]

Sometimes I ask the right questions and offer support and encouragement with words of comfort and hope that emerge from the God in me speaking to the God in them. In every pastoral encounter the chaplain becomes the bearer of a presence, the bearer of a sacred place of God, and these are deeply sacramental moments. I bear witness to my own hope, despair, powerlessness and mortality, and I support others to do the same. By continually working on my own vulnerabilities and the acceptance of myself as a person, I am better placed to enter the vulnerability of others and to be compassionately present.

In many ways the patient becomes the conveyer of all that life can teach you and, in this way, they have nourished my life and ministry. When you experience the inability of people to lose hope or to doubt God in the face of the challenges that life throws at them you can only be inspired. I will never forget words from patients like: 'Nobody will tell me he's not there!'; 'I have no fear, I have God'; 'When I die I will be always be very near to those I love'; or the words of a child after the tragic death of her mother: 'Mammy, I love you more than the size of the bed, more than the size of the hospital, more than the size of the world.' This child knew instinctively that the love she felt for her mother was greater than the loss she felt. To all of us in the Emergency Department that day she was a minster of hope.

Enhanced Well-Being

As a companion profession, we encounter patients who may be facing life-changing surgery, who may have suffered some form of trauma, who are undergoing treatment or are facing an uncertain future. These pastoral encounters may be for a brief phase of the sick person's journey and we fall into step with them for a short time, not as expert but as companion; not as problem-solver but as a listener. This involves accompanying them

---

4   Tim Bennison et al., *Chaplaincy and the Soul of Health and Social Care: Fostering Spiritual Wellbeing in Emerging Paradigms of Care*, London: Jessica Kingsley Publishers, 2019.

in their powerlessness, in their experiencing of strong emotions, in their silences or withdrawals – always with sensitivity to their specific and changing needs. In my experience patients may initially entrust their emotional or spiritual distress to healthcare chaplains rather than burden their families. The outcome of chaplaincy, although not always easy to achieve, is to facilitate the person to articulate whatever would lead to their enhanced well-being of mind, body and spirit.

Cardinal Bernardin, in *A Sign of Hope*,[5] described what patients might need in this way:

> A distinctive goal is not so much to heal [the sickness] better or more efficiently than other health professions, it is to bring care and comfort to people by giving them an experience that will strengthen their confidence in life and give them a reason to hope. In this we find the Christian vocation that makes our healthcare truly distinctive.

Saved by Hope

As well as being a companion, the healthcare chaplaincy profession is also a ministry of hope. In his second encyclical, *Spe Salvi* (*Saved by Hope*), Pope Benedict wrote that, 'God is the foundation of hope, not any god, but the God who has a human face and who has loved us to the end, each one of us, and humanity in its entirety.' Our Christian faith stands by the hope that the ultimate future will be blessed and that sickness and death will not have the last word. Chaplains communicate this hope by knowing and accepting the sacred within themselves, allowing them to authentically practise God's hopeful healing, a hope that is found in Christ (1 Timothy 1:1).

Every day I am both torn and energised by the human reality of sickness and especially by the openness, honesty and generosity of spirit that I encounter. I am also challenged to live my life trusting in God no matter what life throws at me. The sacredness of being a professional

5   Joseph Bernardin, *A Sign of Hope: A Pastoral Letter on Healthcare*, Chicago, IL: Office of Communications, Archdiocese of Chicago, 1995.

companion stepping in for part of a person's journey is captured most clearly by Nicholas Wolterstorff in his 'Lament for a Son':[6]

If you think your task as comforter is to tell me that really,
all things considered, it's not so bad,
you do not sit with me in my grief but place yourself
off in the distance from me.
Over there, you are of no help.
What I need to hear from you is that you recognise how painful it is.
I need to hear from you that you are with me in my desperation.
To comfort me, you have to come close.
Come sit beside me on my mourning bench.

---

6   Nicholas Wolterstorff, *Lament for a Son*, Grand Rapids, MI: William B. Eerdmans Publishing Company, 1987.

19: The Deaf Community

Paddy Boyle

'Be who you are and be that well.'
St Francis De Sales

Memories

I can barely remember when I was not in one way or another connected to the deaf community, particularly to that part of the deaf world associated with the schools in Cabra, St Mary's School for girls and St Joseph's School for boys. When I was five the family moved to the Navan Road, to the outskirts of Dublin city as it was then. The schools for deaf children were just a few fields away. My sisters went to the Dominican primary and secondary schools. For a few years, I attended St Declan's College, just beside St Joseph's School for Deaf Boys. Our annual school retreats were held in the large and very beautiful chapel used by the students of St Joseph's. This chapel is now the Deaf Heritage Centre.

These two orders, the Dominican Sisters and the Christian Brothers, managed the schools until they were amalgamated in 2016 and became the Holy Family School for the Deaf and Hard of Hearing (DHH). The orders ran the schools and were very involved in the pastoral care of their students, not only while they were attending the schools but throughout their lives. One of my sisters was secretary to St Mary's for a number of years and would, on occasion, bring deaf students to our house for dinner. My mother was friendly with a family whose son was deaf and who attended St Joseph's. My mother knew some sign language and often looked after her friend's son after school.

Facilities

Shortly after I was ordained, I was appointed chaplain to the Dominican Sisters in Cabra. The history of this order is truly fascinating, and how they not only became involved in, but were leaders in deaf education from the 1840s until quite recently, is, in itself, a remarkable story. I am friendly with some of the more recent chaplains to the deaf community, Vincentian and diocesan priests and I would often say Mass either in the Sacred Heart Home in Drumcondra or in the Emmaus Chapel in Deaf Village Ireland (DVI), Cabra. I was also invited to deliver a number of talks on scripture topics to groups of deaf people. Whether saying Mass or delivering talks I had, of course, the assistance of competent interpreters. I was always very enriched by these interactions with the deaf and they were real eye-openers for me into issues such as deaf culture, language and communication, and deaf awareness and humour.

When the Dominican Sisters and the Christian Brothers, together with Vincentian priest Fr McNamara and Monsignor William Yore, brought about the establishment of St Mary's in 1846 and St Joseph's in 1857, they were concerned not only for the educational welfare of the students but also for the general and spiritual well-being of deaf children. The various pastoral services that have evolved over time on a basis of need, have become the main concern of the present chaplaincy service.

The Deaf in Christian Tradition

In the Gospel there are very vivid examples of Jesus' interaction with the deaf and hard of hearing (e.g. Mark 7:31–37). While we are not fully knowledgeable of the circumstances of the deaf in the time and society of Jesus, we can be sure that it was marked by exclusion, isolation, marginalisation and discouragement. In his encounter with Jesus the man in Mark's Gospel received back his dignity and his self-esteem, he was reconnected with his peers, his community, and was given the chance to return to his place in society.

One of the threads of concern and involvement with the deaf and hard of hearing, imitating the example of Jesus, can be found in the life of St Francis de Sales, Bishop of Geneva and patron saint of the deaf and hard of hearing. The story of his encounter with Martin, a young deaf man,

171

is well known. Together they developed a language of signs to enable Martin to understand the scriptures and to encounter God and Jesus Christ in the sacraments. Martin found employment and was empowered to live productively and fulfilled in his society and community.

By using signs that he formed with his hands and fingers, St Francis personally began to teach Martin about the Catholic faith. Martin, as was soon clear, was highly intelligent and a very good pupil. After a period of time, through his gentle patience and persistence and with the signs and gestures he had invented for the purpose, St Francis succeeded in instructing Martin about God and His love for all men. All went so well that eventually Martin was able to receive the Holy Eucharist for the first time in 1606. Two years later, Martin was confirmed.

(The National Catholic Office for the Deaf, Washington, DC)

We can still see traces of the French influence in the development of Irish Sign Language (ISL).

Chaplaincy Services

Practically all aspects of the chaplaincy service and of the role and function of a chaplain to the deaf community are to be found in these two narratives. The chaplaincy has at present four chaplains, one ordained and three lay. Included in its vast range of services are liturgical preparation and celebration, advocacy services, visitation, journeying with people at different moments of their lives, and presence in the community.

In recent times there have been enormous changes in society, in religious practice, in education, in modes of communication, in IT and in digital technology. Many of these changes have been very beneficial to the deaf in terms of communication, and avenues of opportunity have opened up that were unimaginable in the not-too-distant past. Without doubt they have also influenced the understanding and methodology of chaplaincy.

Integration

There was a time, not too long ago, when almost all DHH children went to the two schools in Cabra. The schools not only provided an education for deaf children, but they also formed culture, created community, fostered and promoted sign language, sometimes independently of each other. Among the older deaf community men's signs and women's signs are still used. The medical model of deafness was the prevailing one and as such was aligned, in its time, with oralist philosophy, whose day came and went.

Now roughly 95 per cent of DHH children attend mainstream schools. Children are the hope of the community. The children who attend Holy Family School come from a diverse mix of ethnic, religious and national backgrounds. While the school is a Catholic school with a Catholic ethos and provides appropriate religious education, including sacramental preparation and celebration of the sacraments in the Emmaus Chapel, it does make every effort to accommodate children of other faiths and the children of non-religious families. One of the chaplaincy team is chaplain to the school and works in cooperation with the religion teachers in the school.

The Elderly

A significant group of the deaf community are its senior members, mostly past pupils of the two schools. They are in themselves living memories of times gone by, of battles won or lost. They articulate mixed memories of their experiences of the past and glory in aspirations long held dear and now finally fulfilled. They are sure of their place in society and in the deaf community. In a very real sense, they are the soul of the community. They are the ones who regularly attend Mass in the Emmaus Chapel and would have what might be called a very traditional understanding of the chaplaincy. They have a shared history and language. It is in this group you will find the use of men's and women's signs. A sub-group of this cohort are the residents and former residents of the nursing home for deaf and blind-deaf on Brewery Road, Stillorgan. This very special group is in the process of being rehoused in more diverse placements and requires a lot of attention at the moment.

The Young

Finally, there is one other fairly distinct and recognisable group within the deaf community and that is the young deaf, the cohort between twenty and forty. While some are past pupils of the old schools, their influence on them is not as great as it was for the older generations. While they are very much part of the deaf community, they tend to see themselves in a different light from that of the past. They have a social perspective on their history and culture. The enactment of the Irish Sign Language Act on 24 December 2017 has enormous significance for them and, indeed, for all the deaf community.

All the milestone changes in recent years in the mainstreaming of education, the Irish Sign Language Act and huge advancements in technology, have meant the world is a much more open and welcoming environment for the younger deaf person in modern Ireland. Many of them are working in non-traditional employments and, while this is not without its challenges, there are opportunities for them that would not have been dreamt of just a few years ago.

From the point of view of the chaplaincy, the young, as in so many spheres of life, are the heart of the community. They are most receptive and generous in the way they respond to practical challenges. I will give just one among many examples. About thirty years ago, on the Dublin Diocesan Pilgrimage to Lourdes, one of the chaplains to the sick came across a young deaf man. He was non-oral but had sign. The chaplain, who some time later became a chaplain to the deaf, connected the young man to a priest on the pilgrimage who had sign. This priest, who also became a chaplain to the deaf, signed at all the Masses and ceremonies and very kindly looked after the young man for the rest of the pilgrimage. From that one incident the presence and involvement of younger members of the deaf community as pilgrims, as helpers, as leaders, as interpreters etc. has been enormous and significant.

Conclusion
Being a member of the deaf chaplaincy team has been for me a grace-filled and extremely rewarding experience. I have met and worked with some of the most wonderful people you would ever hope to be associated with. May I wish God's bountiful blessing on them all.

Postscript

Alan Hilliard

These past few years I've read quite a number of books on well-being, societal changes and other such subjects. I've noticed that many academics and writers keep a few gems for their final pages, and one of those gems is their religious faith and belief. They ponder on how their faith inspires, nourishes and directs them and how the work of the soul is important in overcoming many of today's problems. For a variety of reasons they cannot include these insights in their main body of work. For whatever reason, God, though not a postscript, has become a postscript.

Chaplains often come across this phenomenon. If they work in secular institutions they are told to hide the 'religious bit', even though it is an integral part of who they are and what they do. One of the world's leading business gurus, Hubert Joly, rediscovered the soul of business through engagements with Catholic monks. Dissatisfied with the emphasis on shareholder profit, he was inspired to take 'a step back and spend time looking into my soul to find a better direction for my life'.[1] Another leading guru in the field of management and business states that the seven most sought-after values in leadership are the seven Cs: 'Complexity, Confidence, Compassion, Care, Courage, Critical Thinking and Communication'.[2] These qualities are not far from what one might describe as the fruits of the Holy Spirit, and are most certainly the fruit of prayer and contemplation.

It is the sincere hope of all involved in this publication that you found time to reflect on the issues surrounding chaplaincy in Part Two and that you enjoyed the journey with those who work in diverse chaplaincy

---

1 Hubert Joly with Caroline Lambert, *The Heart of Business: Leadership Principles for the Next Era of Capitalism*, Brighton, MA: Harvard Business Review Press, 2021, 17.
2 Manfred F. R. Kets de Vries, *The CEO Whisperer* (The Palgrave Kets de Vries Library), Cham, Switzerland: Springer International Publishing (Kindle edition), 11.

settings in Part Three. The book does not seek to be conclusive on the role of chaplaincy or its definition but seeks to honour how it is understood, manifested and reflected on by those who are directly involved in this work of hope. There are aspects that require further reflection. Tensions and questions emerge throughout. One could ponder whether and if chaplaincy is solely about one-to-one engagement or a force for systemic change in various settings. Furthermore, the question as to who mandates the work, mission and personnel is also opened up, not to mention the enormous range of skills and experience necessary in the execution of the role. There is no doubt that chaplaincy in Ireland and in many countries throughout the world demands increasing diversity. Ministry in these settings will only be successful if each and every person shows respect towards the ethos and values of those they work alongside. Hopefully this book will help those from other faith and belief systems to understand the mindset of those who minister from a Catholic perspective.

The life of a Christian minister is fundamentally one of reflection – reflection that leads to action and transformation. A faith that imbues all that we do can transform people and the world. This book brings attention to the dynamic and energetic work of the Holy Spirit that is ministered by ordinary humble people who seek only to serve. They take on a mantle, not of authority, but of service, in a role known to us as 'chaplain'. This book is a testament to the real and lasting hope that this role brings in daily engagements. We trust that it has brought you the self-same hope that many experience when they encounter the presence of the beginning and end of all – Christ, the Alpha and Omega – in one another. Chaplaincy reveals God and his Son Jesus as utter gratuity – a gift to our world and to our lives. He is not a postscript, but One who is at the heart of life and all being.

The Contributors

- Ronan Barry works for the Spiritan Education Trust with responsibility for areas of ethos within the Spiritan network. Previously, he worked as a school chaplain in the network. Ronan's professional career has spanned many different areas within the community and formal education sectors but he has always worked within value-led organisations. Ronan and his wife Joanne have three children.

- Catherine Black has been a member of the chaplaincy team in Mountjoy Male Prison since 2018. She studied at St Patrick's College Maynooth, graduating with a Bachelor of Theology in 2005 and a Masters of Pastoral Studies in 2007. In 2016–17 Catherine took part in the RTÉ documentary series *Ministry of Hope*, which followed her chaplaincy ministry in Shelton Abbey open prison. Catherine, originally from Strabane in County Tyrone, is married and lives in County Wexford.

- Fr Paddy Boyle is a priest of the Archdiocese of Dublin and chaplain to the Deaf Community, Administrator of St Monica's Parish, Edenmore, and St Benedict's, Grange Park.

- Fr John Campion SDB is a member of the chaplaincy team at the University of Limerick. He has ministered at Pallaskenry Agricultural College and at Our Lady Help of Christians Parish, Milford, Castletroy. John is a member of the Salesian provincial leadership team.

- Gráinne Delaney studied at Mater Dei Institute and has been school chaplain in Crescent College Comprehensive SJ for over twenty years. During this time she has also worked as Co-ordinator of School Ethos. She is a member of the Ignatian Formation Group for Jesuit Schools and the Jesuit European Network (JECSE).

- Rev. Dr Eugene Duffy, a priest of the Diocese of Achonry, is a lecturer in Theology and Religious Studies at Mary Immaculate College, University of Limerick; he is a co-moderator of the Peter and Paul Seminar, and Vicar for Pastoral Renewal and Development in the Diocese of Achonry.

- Fr Hugh Gillan OH has been a St John of God brother for over fifty years. He graduated as a psychiatric nurse in 1971. In 1972 he was appointed to minister in the province services in Korea and remained there for almost twenty-four years. He returned to Ireland to study for the priesthood and was ordained in October 2000. He was then appointed as chaplain in St John of God Hospital, Stillorgan, County Dublin, where he is still ministering.

- Rev. Dr Thomas G. Grenham SPS is currently Assistant Professor of Chaplaincy Studies and Religious Education in the School of Human Development, Institute of Education, Dublin City University. He was formerly the Director of Undergraduate Programmes and Head of Theology at All Hallows College, Dublin City University, Dublin. He has lectured in religious education at Mary Immaculate College, University of Limerick. He was the former Associate Dean for Student Affairs and Head of the Department of Pastoral Theology at the Milltown Institute of Philosophy and Theology, Dublin. He served as a missionary for many years among the Turkana of Kenya (1985–95) and is a member of St Patrick's Missionary Society, Kiltegan, County Wicklow.

- Karla Clarke Hanley lives in County Wicklow with her husband and her two children, who she considers to be their most wonderful achievement. She has a BA in Business Studies and loves looking after her children, reading, swimming, cycling and walking the family dog. Fr Gerry celebrated her wedding twenty-one years ago and remained a close friend.

- Fr Alan Hilliard is Co-ordinator of the Pastoral Care and Chaplaincy Service at TU Dublin. He is a writer and a regular contributor to *The Sacred Heart Messenger* magazine and RTÉ's *A Word in Edgeways*. He is priest of the Archdiocese of Dublin.

- Sr Susan Jones CHF is in ministry in TU Dublin on the Blanchardstown Campus. She has spent several years as chaplain to the homeless community in Depaul, Dublin, where she still volunteers. She is also a volunteer with the Ignatian Spirituality Project, which works to offer spiritual companionship and hope to men and women who are homeless and in recovery from addiction.

- Fr John Kelly, a priest of the Archdiocese of Dublin, studied at Holy Cross College, Clonliffe, Marino Institute of Education and the Royal College of Surgeons Ireland Institute of Leadership. He is Director of Pastoral Care at Tallaght University Hospital, Chair of the Dublin Roman Catholic Hospital Chaplains Association, Chair of the Healthcare Chaplaincy Board and a member of the Council for Health of the Irish Catholic Bishops's Conference.

- Sr Anna Kennedy DC was a registered nurse before entering the community of the Daughters of Charity. She practised nursing in North Infirmary, Cork, the Rotunda Hospital, Dublin, Our Lady's Hospital for Sick Children, Dublin, rural health centres in Nigeria and famine relief in Ethiopia. In 2003 Sr Anna completed a master's degree in healthcare chaplaincy at Mater Dei Institute of Education, Dublin, and took on the role of healthcare chaplain in St Francis Hospice (2001–20)

- Fr John McCarthy is a priest of the Diocese of Limerick. He is a member of the Irish Catholic Bishops' Council for Emigrants and Prisoners Overseas and he worked for many years as chaplain to the Irish community in Boston.

- Rev. Dr Ciarán O'Carroll is a parish priest in the Dublin Archdiocese. Formerly rector of the Pontifical Irish College in Rome, he holds a doctorate in ecclesiastical history and has taught ecclesiastical history at a variety of Catholic colleges and institutes.

- Sr Eileen O'Connell OP is from Cork and now lives in Belfast. She holds a master's degree in theology (Sacred Scripture) from St Patrick's College Maynooth and is engaged in a variety of ministries.

- Sr Siobhán O'Keeffe SSHJM is a Registered General Nurse and holds a master's degree in applied theology, justice, peace and mission from the Missionary Institute London. A diploma in person-centred dementia care allows her to offer spirituality and dementia care training to religious communities and parishes in the UK and Ireland. She has worked as a Marie Curie STARS nurse caring for the terminally ill and their families at home. She works as an envoy for the Medaille Trust, a charity that supports people who are victims of human trafficking, and she is the author of a number of books on prayer and spirituality.

- Sr Sarah O'Rourke FMA worked as a primary school teacher and principal before joining the UL chaplaincy team. Sarah has trained as a spiritual director and in bereavement support. She is a member of the Salesian Sisters' provincial leadership team.

- James M. Sheehan FRCSI, PhD, FAEI is a retired orthopaedic consultant and founder of the Blackrock Clinic.

- Mgr Eoin Thynne was ordained to the priesthood in 1984 and appointed as teacher/chaplain to Maynooth Post-Primary School. In 1990 he was appointed chaplain to Cathal Brugha Barracks, Rathmines, Dublin, and became Head Chaplain to the Defence Forces in 2005. He is currently administrator in the Parish of St Luke the Evangelist in Mulhuddart, Tyrrelstown, Hollystown, Dublin.